How to Pray With the Bible

The Ancient Prayer Form of
Lectio Divina Made Simple

OTHER WORKS BY KARL A. SCHULTZ

The Art and Vocation of Caring for Persons in Pain. Mahwah, N.J.: Paulist Press, 1994.

Bearing the Unbearable: Coping with Infertility and Other Intimate Suffering: Biblical Meditations and Contemporary Applications Using Lectio Divina. Ann Arbor, Mich.: Nimble Books, 2007.

Becoming Community: Biblical Meditations and Applications in Modern Life. New York: New City Press, 2007.

The Bible and You (with Loreen Hanley Duquin). Huntington, Ind.: Our Sunday Visitor, 2004.

Calming the Stormy Seas of Stress. Winona, Minn.: St. Mary's Press, 1998.

The How-To Book of the Bible. Huntington, Ind.: Our Sunday Visitor, 2004.

Job Therapy. Pittsburgh: Genesis Personal Development Center, 1996.

Journaling with Moses and Job. Boston: St. Paul Books and Media, 1996.

Nourished by the Word: A Dialogue with Brother Andrew Campbell, O.S.B., on Praying the Scriptures and Holistic Personal Growth (audiocassette). Notre Dame, Ind.: Ave Maria Press, 1994.

Personal Energy Management: A Christian Personal and Professional Development Program. Chicago: Loyola University Press, 1994.

Personal Energy Manager Rainbow Planner™, Pittsburgh: Genesis Personal Development Center, 1996.

Pope Paul VI: Christian Virtues and Values. New York: Crossroad Publishing Company, 2007.

Where Is God When You Need Him?: Sharing Stories of Suffering With Job and Jesus. Staten Island, N.Y.: Alba House, 1992.

How to Pray With the Bible

The Ancient Prayer Form of *Lectio Divina* Made Simple

KARL A. SCHULTZ

Our Sunday Visitor Publishing Division
Our Sunday Visitor, Inc.
Huntington, Indiana 46750

Copyright © 2007 by Our Sunday Visitor Publishing Division, Our Sunday Visitor, Inc. Published 2007
12 11 10 09 08 07   1 2 3 4 5 6 7 8 9

Our Sunday Visitor Publishing Division
Our Sunday Visitor, Inc.
200 Noll Plaza
Huntington, IN 46750

ISBN: 978-1-59276-216-3 (Inventory No. T267)
LCCN: 2006940663

Cover design by Tyler Ottinger
Cover photo courtesy of Shutterstock.com
Interior design by Sherri L. Hoffman

PRINTED IN THE UNITED STATES OF AMERICA

With love, always:

To my mother and father,
who nurtured me in the faith through word
and especially example and love.

KARL

Acknowledgments

I am grateful to Rev. Timothy Fitzgerald, C.P., for his guidance and support. Joan Cowen was helpful in my early days of wrestling with the Bible. I am grateful to the teachers, coaches, and administration at my grade school, St. Sebastian's in Pittsburgh, and particularly Frank Naderhoff, who taught me the fundamentals of reading, grammar, discipline, and history. My fervor and intuition for the Bible and Catholicism was stoked by the enthusiasm and support of Frank Cambria at St. Mary's Student Parish in Ann Arbor, Mich. I appreciate Red Cully's compassion, guidance, encouragement, and moral support, going far beyond the gridiron. And I will always be beholden and grateful to the one who introduced me to *lectio divina* and supported me in my vocation and profession.

I appreciate the efforts of my editors, Richard Beemer and George Foster, and Michael Dubruiel's support, flexibility, and commitment to *lectio divina*.

Table of Contents

Introduction

"Inner silence is necessary to listen to the Word of God, to experience His presence, to hear God's call. Today our psychology is turned outward too much. The exterior scene is so absorbing that our attention is mainly directed outside; we are nearly always absent from our personal abode. We are unable to meditate, unable to pray. We are unable to silence the hubbub inside, due to outside interests, images, passions. There is no quiet, holy space in the heart for the flame of Pentecost.

We pretend, perhaps, to have special "charisms" in order to claim blind autonomy for the spiritual caprices of our instincts, and we do not try to bring back our feelings and thoughts to the authentic phase of divine inspiration.

The conclusion follows automatically: We must give inner life its place in the program of our busy existence; a primary place, a silent place, a pure place. We must find ourselves again in order to be fit to have the life-bringing and sanctifying Spirit in us. If not, how can we listen to His "testimony"? (cf. Jn 15:26; Rom 8:7).

— POPE PAUL VI, PENTECOST, MAY 21, 1972

THE BIBLE'S VERSATILITY

The Bible is the story of humankind. It is a diverse collection of seventy-three books written over the course of a millennium in a wide range of cultural and political environments. It contains various literary styles and distinct theological and anthropological perspectives (ways of looking at God and humanity). As Thomas Merton observed, its breadth and universality make it humanity's book as well as the Church's.

The Bible's authorship is a joint venture between God and humanity, which makes it unique in world literature. While its primary purpose is religious, it is also suited to other approaches and objectives. It has compelling historical, psychological, sociological, literary, motivational, and aesthetic applications that complement its spirituality.

The Bible has inspired some of the greatest art, drama, literature, and music the world has known. It has been analyzed and utilized by some of the world's most prominent psychiatrists and psychologists (e.g., Carl Jung, Viktor Frankl, Paul Tournier, Karl Menninger, Conrad W. Baars, Adrian van Kaam). Politicians and social activists have used and abused it in ways that have changed the course of history. The civil rights movement in the United States had roots in biblical spirituality, particularly the motif of the Hebrews' exodus from Egypt.

PRAYING WITH THE BIBLE

Essential to the Bible's religious dimension are prayer and corresponding actions. This book is specifically concerned with "praying with the Bible." How is that different from prayer per se, or from reading the Bible? Is it a hybrid? Is the difference between "praying the Bible" and "praying with the Bible? (this book's title) substantive or semantics?

Let's begin with a definition of purpose. The objective of praying with the Bible is to dialogue with God and be taught, healed, and transformed by the encounter. The next and most important step is to live it.

Much of our communication with God is non-verbal. The Holy Spirit knows the language of the heart. Just as couples find contentment in resting in the silence of each other's company, likewise when we pray with the Bible we reach a point of simply lingering silently with the Lord and basking receptively in His presence. Praying encompasses more than saying formal prayers. It is God and the praying persons communicating and offering themselves to one another.

Faith and prayer express themselves through works of love: "If any one says, 'I love God,' and hates his brother, he is a liar; for he who does not love his brother whom he has seen, cannot love God whom he has not seen" (1 Jn 4:20; cf. Jas 2:14-17). As conveyed throughout the Sermon on the Mount (cf. Mt 5-7), and particularly in its conclusion, our subsequent actions reveal our prayers' substance and fruitfulness. Accordingly, this book is not only about how to pray with the Bible, but how to bring it to life.

PRAYING THE BIBLE

Praying the Bible is a more narrow approach to the Bible. We are primarily concerned with praying it, as opposed to reflecting upon or studying it. We relive the biblical experience by entering into it imaginatively and spiritually, and praying about it. Obviously there is some overlap with praying with the Bible, for prayer involves some level of reflection and interpretation in order to make sense of the passage and utilize it as a means of prayer.

Sometimes when we pray with the Bible (in particular, the Psalms) we are simply praying the Bible. There is much crossover between the two, but the distinction remains.

Using the Bible as a prayer book has been part of Christian spirituality from the beginning. The book of Psalms was intended primarily to facilitate prayer.

Although the difference is subtle, I prefer using the conjunction "with" in reference to praying the Bible because it implies a joint venture, not only with the composers and original audiences of the Bible, but with all believers.

As Karl Barth observed, Christians should have the Bible in one hand and the newspaper in the other. God has involved himself intimately in human affairs, and He wishes us to be His hands and feet. To do so properly, we need biblically inspired prayer in the context of the life of the Church (i.e., the sacraments, devotions, service, and Christian fellowship). This book will provide a spirituality model suitable to such.

To remind us of the guidance the magisterium provides in understanding and applying Sacred Scripture, each chapter begins with a papal reflection or exhortation on the Bible. To remind us of the effort and creativity we must exercise in order to be fruitful recipients of the Word, and to make our learning concrete as well as conceptual, each chapter ends with simple but challenging spiritual exercises identified as Prayer Possibilities — the name matching the nature of the activities as well as the mnemonic (memory-jarring) "P" alliteration of the icons discussed below.

WHOM THIS BOOK IS FOR

This book is for those who wish to deepen their relationship with God through prayerful reading and living of the Bible. It does not presume familiarity with the Bible, and is written at a basic level. It will likewise be helpful for persons with an advanced understanding of Scripture who wish to engage it in holistic prayer as well as study, and for persons who teach Scripture and spirituality to others.

WHAT THIS BOOK IS ABOUT

You will learn guidelines for praying with the Bible according to the Church's ancient and most widely utilized biblical spirituality model, *lectio divina* (sacred reading). I will integrate the wisdom of the Bible, Tradition, the magisterium (the authoritative teachings of the popes and bishops), and the faithful (the person in the pew), while also sharing my own insights and experience.

We will explore *lectio divina's* historical background and evolution, recent guidelines and exhortations offered by the Church, and its practice by believers. I will offer reflection questions and applications designed to help you discover *lectio divina's* and the Bible's intimate and pervasive connection with your life.

In the Bible, God acted in human history on both an individual and communal level, and continues to do so. *Lectio divina* is a natural framework for bringing the Bible to life in the dual sense of making it come alive and relating it to life.

THE BIBLE AND LIFE

Prayer, the Bible, and life go together. God acts and speaks to us in life and the Bible, and both evoke prayer.

Praying with the Bible is an ongoing, dynamic, organic activity, rather than something we relegate to quiet time independent of the essential content and direction of our life. Thus, even though you may not be well versed in the Bible, you have life experience, which contributes significantly to a proper biblical interpretation, assimilation, application, and response.

The Bible is about each of us. It is our story. It is both timeless and time-conditioned. Parallels to and applications of its characters, events, circumstances, and teachings occur in our lives through the mystery of divine providence.

Praying with the Bible and discerning and responding to God's initiative in our life feed off each other. The Catholic model we will explore, *lectio divina*, is more than a spiritual activity; it is a way of life, communication, and personal and communal transformation.

The following is my favorite commentary on the Bible's correspondence to life. It can serve as a spiritual foundation for our exploration. It comes from *Through Moses to Jesus*, by Cardinal Carlo Maria Martini, S.J., emeritus archbishop of Milan, a renowned biblical scholar, ecumenical leader, and promoter of *lectio divina*:

"In the history of Moses, as in the other events recorded in the Bible, we find realities that are repeated in the life of every individual. Anyone who is inwardly open and acquainted with prayer can find in the words of Scripture what is needed for his or her life.

"It seems to me that the decisive questions to be asked by each person are:

- What does this Scripture passage mean to me?
- What is it saying to me?
- How is it related to my life?

"We might at first say, "It doesn't have anything to do with my life." But rather than remain with such a first impression, we should look for the cause and ask, "Why is there no connection between this Bible passage and my life? What would I want the connection to be?"

"In this way, even a negative first impression can be a means of contact between what the Bible says and what we experience. Often this contact does not take place immediately, but only after we have entered into a dialogue, a wrestling with the words of Scripture. Only then does it begin to shed light.

"Such a dialogue is a decisive help toward prayer, which springs from our center and expresses our deepest yearnings. This is the aim of spiritual guidance: To help us express ourselves in prayer as we are, in keeping with our situation and nature.

"Real prayer is not child's play. Scripture teaches us that prayer is a struggle, a battle. It places us face-to-face with our greatest difficulties. In prayer we are trained to look at the problems of our life with an open eye and to accept them, for human beings are often afraid to confront themselves."

PRAYING WITH ICONS

In a religious context, icons are sacred images designed to inspire prayer and adoration. In a contemporary educational, computer, or literary context the term describes explanatory, transparent pictures that communicate meaning or function. Our usage will bridge these definitions. The icons in this book are as follows:

"Prayer Pointers" include practical directives, suggestions, and opportunities for praying with the Bible.

"Prayer Passages" indicate biblical passages or other spiritual literature that illuminate the subject.

"Prayer Particulars" are insights, personal experiences, and background information that facilitate deeper comprehension and contextual, contemporary, and personal understanding of the Bible and *lectio divina*. In some cases, these may be of a detailed and specific nature, so if you prefer a more general discussion, feel free to skip them for the moment and perhaps return to them later.

"Prayer Ponderings" are reflection questions and spiritual exercises designed to facilitate personal assimilation and application of key concepts and practices.

TRANSLATION USED AND BIBLICAL ABBREVIATIONS

When quoting the Bible, this book uses the Revised Standard Version, Catholic Edition, because it is both literal and accessible (i.e., comprehensible to persons without a background in the Bible). You do not need to use the same translation to follow along.

The New American Bible (which is used in the American liturgy and lectionary), The New Jerusalem Bible, and the New Revised Standard Version, Catholic Edition, are other fine Catholic translations. See *The How-To Book of the Bible* (Our Sunday Visitor) for a more extensive discussion of translation characteristics and differences.

I reference biblical passages throughout the book not only as a basis and justification for my comments, but also to familiarize you with the Bible and opportunities for practicing *lectio divina*. Life experience, practice, and book learning are complementary and synergistic. For flow and space reasons, I frequently provide biblical cross-references (i.e., citations such as Jn 2 or 1 Cor 12) rather than direct quotations.

Following is the system commonly used for referencing the Bible. Abbreviations of biblical books vary slightly by translation, but are easy to decipher. They can be found in your Bible's table of contents.

DECIPHERING A BIBLICAL REFERENCE

- A biblical reference begins with the abbreviation of the biblical book, e.g., Gen for Genesis. The abbreviation is not followed by a period. (An older, decreasingly used, referencing system includes a period after the abbreviation and in lieu of colons, for example, Gen. 1.1).
- A number before the abbreviation indicates the first, second, or third book of that name. For example, 3 Jn refers to the third letter of John, and 2 Cor refers to the second letter of St. Paul to the Corinthians.
- After the biblical abbreviation comes the chapter. For example, Mk 5 refers to the fifth chapter of Mark.
- If the reference points to a specific verse(s), it will continue with a colon, then the verse number. For example, Ruth 2:4 means the fourth verse of chapter two of Ruth.

- A series of verses within the same chapter are designated by a hyphen. For example, Num 4:1-7 means verses one through seven of the fourth chapter of Numbers.
- A sequence of chapters within the same book are also designated by a hyphen. Jn 13-17 refers to the thirteenth through seventeenth chapters of the Gospel of John. Remember, a colon is necessary to designate a verse.
- Commas separate discontinuous verses within the same chapter. For example, Lk 3:1, 6, 7 means the first, sixth, and seventh verses of chapter three of Luke's Gospel.
- Semicolons distinguish different chapters. For example, Eccl 3:7; 5:8, means the seventh verse of chapter three of Ecclesiastes and the eighth verse of chapter five. Deut 3; 7; 9 means the third, seventh, and ninth chapters of Deuteronomy. Remember, a colon is necessary to indicate a verse.
- If more than one biblical book is referenced, it will be contained in a separate designation and separated by a semicolon, for example, Jn 3:3; Ps 1:2.
- Decipher this one: Lk 4:5-8; 3:4, 6; 10:1. It refers to the Gospel of Luke, verses five through eight of chapter four, verses four and six of chapter three, and verse one of chapter ten.
- The letters "f." or "ff." following a biblical reference means the verse(s) designated and those that follow. Scholars use this with the assumption that their reader will know from the context how far to read.
- The term "cf." means cross-reference, and precedes a passage(s) that is referenced but not quoted. If a passage is quoted verbatim, its reference will not be preceded by a "cf."
- When a reference ends in a, b, or c, it refers to the first, second, or third part of a verse that is lengthy or reflects

a break in thought. Such detail occurs mostly in scholarly writings.

- Occasionally we encounter passages in which the chapter and verse designations do not accurately reflect breaks in the text. It is the biblical text that is inspired, not the verse numbering system, which came more than a millennium after the final book of the Bible was written.
- Gen 2:4 illustrates both of the above. The first half of the verse, identified as Gen 2:4a, concludes the first creation story (Gen 1:1-2:4a), and the second half of the verse, Gen 2:4b, begins the second creation story (Gen 2:4b-3:24).

FEEDBACK

Your feedback contributes significantly to the refinement of my faith and message. I welcome your insights, stories, and suggestions. You can contact me on my Web site (www.karlaschultz.com), e-mail me at karlaschultz@juno.com, or write to me at Genesis Personal Development Center, 3431 Gass Avenue, Pittsburgh, PA 15212-2239. The telephone number is (412) 766-7545.

Chapter One

——*Lectio Divina*: The Church's Way —— of Praying With the Bible

> Today it is recognized as a general need of Christian piety that every form of worship should have a biblical imprint. The progress made in biblical studies, the increasing dissemination of the Sacred Scriptures, and above all the example of Tradition and the interior action of the Holy Spirit are tending to cause the modern Christian to use the Bible ever increasingly as the basic prayerbook, and to draw from it genuine inspiration and unsurpassable examples.
>
> — POPE PAUL VI, MARIALIS CULTIS, "ON THE RIGHT ORDERING AND DEVELOPMENT OF DEVOTION TO THE BLESSED VIRGIN MARY," 30

Biblically based prayer is at the core of the Church's spirituality. It has a personal, communal, and liturgical dimension, and permeates the Mass and the Church's devotional life.

Because prayer is a simple, fundamental, and natural activity, there is no need for complex theories or esoteric jargon, and you will encounter none in this book. Praying with the Bible is a dialogue whose objective is not agenda fulfillment and achievement, but rather awareness, acceptance, assimilation, and actualization of God's word and providence, that is, His will and plan for us. It is more about sharing ourselves and responding to God's call/initiative and life's challenges than scrupulously following a technique or method.

This book will help you recognize the continuity between prayer and action and between the Bible and life. As you become familiar with the Catholic model for praying with the Bible, you will realize that much of it is already part of your experience.

The Bible can transform us and our relationship with God. This is the purpose of the simple, enjoyable, and challenging ancient prayer form known as *lectio divina*.

LECTIO DIVINA

Lectio divina (often abbreviated to *lectio*) is Latin for "divine reading." It is one of the few Latin expressions remaining in the Catholic vernacular. Its linguistic longevity can be attributed to tradition, habit, and the inability of translations to convey its rich meaning. As you will discover, *lectio divina* is a dynamic type of reading that exceeds the common understanding of the term.

Lectio divina is composed of five main activities: reading/listening, meditation, prayer, contemplation, and action. Its components have varied over the years. The model has evolved in accordance with the pastoral needs and theological development of the Church and the movement of the Holy Spirit. The following chart previews both traditional and contemporary articulations of *lectio divina* along with the "School of the Word" model developed and promoted by Cardinal Martini and discussed below.

PREPARING FOR OUR ENCOUNTER WITH THE LORD

The first stage in the contemporary model of relax, retreat, and renew takes into account the hyperactivity and intensity of modern persons, families, and communities, and it recognizes the importance of easing into an encounter with the Lord, just as we would with a dinner guest at our home. Unless we want to make our guest and perhaps ourselves uncomfortable and defensive, we

Traditional	Contemporary	School of the Word
	Relax, Retreat, Renew	
Lectio (Reading / Listening)	Reading / Listening / Sensing	Reading
Meditatio (Meditation)	Repetition, Rumination, Reflection, Reminiscence	Meditation
Oratio (Prayer)	Prayer (Active Dialogue)	Prayer
Contemplatio (Contemplation)	Contemplation (Receptive Dialogue)	Contemplation
		Discernment
		Decision
		Consolation
Operatio (Action)	Action	Action

don't immediately dive into a deep or potentially conflictual discussion. We give ourselves time to acclimate to the environment and person and let go of peripheral issues and potential distractions, and gradually build up to a level of disclosure that we feel comfortable with.

Likewise, it is helpful to allow ourselves time to slow down from our frantic pace, take temporary leave of our temporal concerns, and prepare ourselves mentally, physiologically (e.g., by deep breathing or relaxation exercises designed to help us calm down, center ourselves, and enter into the present more fully), emotionally, and spiritually for an intimate encounter with the Lord.

This preparation is similar to praying or reading the lectionary readings prior to Mass in order to dispose ourselves more fully to meet Jesus in His Word, Body and Blood, and community.

MAGISTERIAL PRONOUNCEMENTS AND INITIATIVES

Led by Scripture scholar and retired Archbishop of Milan Cardinal Martini, the magisterium has recently intensified its promotion of *lectio*. It is important to be aware of significant Church documents and organizations designed to foster biblical spirituality. Familiarity with these reveals that *lectio divina* (often abbreviated to *lectio*) is the Catholic Church's official model for prayerfully reading the Scriptures:

- It is referred to implicitly through the terms "reading and prayer" (the early Church's way of describing what would come to be known as *lectio*) in Vatican Council II's Dogmatic Constitution on Divine Revelation, also known as *Dei Verbum* (which means "the Word of God").

- One of the most important magisterial initiatives undertaken in response to *Dei Verbum* was Pope Paul VI's inauguration of the Catholic Biblical Federation in 1969. The chief architect and point man for its implementation was Cardinal Augustin Bea, former rector of the Pontifical Biblical Institute and one of the most prominent biblical scholars in the world. He was ably followed by Cardinal Johannes Willebrands, who, like Cardinal Bea, was a former president of the Secretariat for Promoting Christian Unity. Not coincidentally, those in the Church who have been active in the biblical renewal are also typically involved in ecumenism because, when understood properly, the word of God unites believers.

    Through its resources, publications, and conferences, the Catholic Biblical Federation has become an international promoter of biblical spirituality and ministry in the life of individuals and the local and universal Church. Its Web site, c-b-f.org, contains helpful materials on *lectio divina* and other aspects of biblical spirituality and ministry, including papers and transcripts of speeches from the Federation's International Congress on *Dei Verbum*, which was held at the Vatican September 14-18, 2005. Also available on the Web site is information on the bishops' synod on "The Word of God in the Life and Mission of the Church," scheduled to be held at the Vatican October 5-26, 2008.

- *Lectio divina* is discussed explicitly in the Pontifical Biblical Commission's (PBC) 1993 document, "The Interpretation of the Bible in the Church" (II, A) and in the Catholic *Catechism of the Catholic Church* (nos. 1177, 2708). The PBC document identifies *lectio divina* as both an individual and communal activity, and does not recommend any other model of biblical spirituality.

- In his 1999 apostolic exhortation *Ecclesia in America* ("The Church in America"), Pope John Paul II wrote:

" 'I am the Way, the Truth and the Life' (Jn 14:6). With these words, Jesus presents himself as the one path which leads to holiness. But a specific knowledge of this way comes chiefly through the Word of God which the Church proclaims in her preaching. Therefore, the Church in America 'must give a clear priority to prayerful reflection on Sacred Scripture by all the faithful' (*Propositio* 32). This reading of the Bible, accompanied by prayer, is known in the tradition of the Church as *lectio divina*, and it is a practice to be encouraged among all Christians. For priests, the *lectio divina* must be a basic feature of the preparation of their homilies, especially the Sunday homily (cf. John Paul II, Apostolic Letter *Dies Domini* [May 31, 1998], 40: AAS 90 [1998], 738)."

- In his address to the attendees at the 2005 Catholic Biblical Federation conference at the Vatican, Pope Benedict offered the most extensive and enthusiastic endorsement of *lectio* of any modern pontiff:

"In this context, I would like in particular to recall and recommend the ancient tradition of *Lectio divina*: the diligent reading of Sacred Scripture accompanied by prayer brings about that intimate dialogue in which the person reading hears God who is speaking, and in

---

PRAYER PASSAGES

 "You will have noticed that much has been said about Holy Scripture since the Council. References appear everywhere in the Council's documents, but they are most frequent in the Constitution on the Sacred Liturgy (cf. nos. 24, 33, 35, 51...), in the Constitution on the Church (cf. nos. 6, 15, 24...), and in the Decree on Ecumenism (no. 21). If we tried to list them all, we should never finish.

"A most important document was deliberately devoted to Holy Scripture itself. That document is the Dogmatic Constitution on Divine Revelation, which is called *Dei Verbum*, from the words with which it begins. It is one of the Council's most weighty documents. It may be described as a fundamental one, together with those on the Church (*Lumen gentium*) and on the relationship between the Church and the world (*Gaudium et spes*).

"It outlines the doctrinal process that has gone on in the Church since the Council of Trent.

"It indicates the weightiest biblical problems that have arisen in these latter times.

"It establishes the function of Holy Scripture in respect to Revelation, namely, that it takes God's Word down in writing (cf. *Dei Verbum*, 7), and it defines its relationship with Tradition (nos. 8-9).

"It states its relation to the Church's magisterium (no. 10), that is to say, to the rule of faith." (Pope Paul VI, July 1, 1970)

---

praying, responds to him with trusting openness of heart (cf. *Dei Verbum*, n. 25). If it is effectively promoted, this practice will bring to the Church — I am convinced of it — a new spiritual springtime.

"As a strong point of biblical ministry, *Lectio divina* should therefore be increasingly encouraged, also through the use of new methods, carefully thought through and in step with the times. It should never be forgotten that the Word of God is a lamp for our feet and a light for our path (cf. Ps 119[118]: 105)." (Pope Benedict XVI, address to the Catholic Biblical Federation's International Congress on *Dei Verbum*, September 16, 2005.)

LECTIO DIVINA'S REVIVAL

The above is an example of the magisterium's renewed commitment to the promotion of *lectio divina* and its status as both a traditional and cutting-edge spirituality within the Church. Such biblically driven spirituality is essential in today's secular environment. As theologian Karl Rahner pointed out, a Christian in the new millennium will have to be a mystic in order to remain a Christian.

As is often the case in the Church, *lectio divina's* modern rebirth began at the grassroots level. *Too Deep for Words: Rediscovering Lectio Divina*, a book published by Paulist Press in 1988 by a Cenacle sister, Thelma Hall, was one of the first titles to catch on with the laity. For the last two decades, the practice of *lectio divina* has steadily increased in both first- and third-world countries.

Lectio divina has always been a staple of the Church's spirituality. Religious communities and movements have customized *lectio* to their needs and circumstances. Terminology, emphases, and styles have evolved, but the activities and objectives have remained essentially the same.

LECTIO DIVINA'S PRE-CHRISTIAN ROOTS AND UNIVERSAL NATURE

Lectio divina is the oldest and most natural model for interacting holistically (with our whole selves: body, mind, and spirit) with God's word. Its roots predate not only Christianity, but even Judaism, so we should not approach it in a possessive and sectarian (viewing it as Catholic in exclusive rather than inclusive terms) manner. It is a Catholic, but also catholic, (i.e., universal) activity, and therefore we can confidently share it with others without imposing our beliefs on them. It can foster respectful, non-threatening, ecumenical dialogue.

I have shared the *lectio* process with Jews, Muslims, Orthodox, and Protestants, and they have noted similarities to their own practices of spiritual reading. Pious Jews "doven" (i.e., read from their *siddur* [prayer book] while rocking back and forth [referred to as *shukkling*, and representative of the holistic energy generated by contact with God and His Word] and following the biblical words with their finger).

When Muslims gather to read the Koran, they sometimes engage in what they refer to as a circle study. While sitting facing one another in a circle as a symbol of equality and mutual respect, they read the text aloud, have a period of silence, and then discuss it, usually in response to reflections by a group leader.

These common practices should not be surprising, as the three great Western religions have common geographical and historical origins.

Although *lectio divina's* primary pre-Christian development occurred primarily within Judaism, it also has roots in the reading practices of earlier oral cultures, extending as far back as Sumer, located in what is now Southern Iraq. Because of its advances in writing, commerce, and culture, most historians and archaeologists regard Sumer as the first civilization.

I mention *lectio's* historical roots in recognition of its timeless and universal relevance. The ancient Hebrews and early Christians did not manufacture *lectio divina*. The term should be understood as a description of the natural way human beings holistically interact with a religious text, and by relation, a life experience or interpersonal encounter.

JEWISH ORIGINS

The Jewish origins of *lectio divina* can be traced to the oral communication practices that preceded and underlie the written Word of the Bible. Even as the Jews gradually moved to a written culture, they continued to use many of the principles and practices developed during the oral stage of the biblical tradition. This included reciting the biblical texts aloud, repeating them for emphasis, memorization, and assimilation, and oscillating between personal application (relating the Word to their life so that it was experienced as dynamic and personal), emotional response, supplication (petition for help), and quiet receptivity.

Typically, this was done in a liturgical (worship), clan, or familial setting. Individual spirituality is a later development within the Old Testament that was fueled first by the later prophetic writings (particularly Ezekiel and Jeremiah) and then the wisdom literature (e.g., Job, Proverbs, Sirach, and Ecclesiastes, which primarily function as guidance on moral and prudential living). When the Babylonians destroyed Jerusalem and its temple and deported most of the Jewish survivors in 587 B.C., Israel's spirituality shifted in focus from temple worship to the word of God, which of course was more conducive to individual spirituality. During and immediately after the Babylonian exile, the Torah, the first five books of the Old Testament, began to take their final form, and other books of the Bible were refined and disseminated.

However, the sense of collective responsibility remained strong, and thus it was most common for the Bible to be heard in a group. Even those few individuals who were literate and affluent enough to have texts available to them (although most memorized them) experienced them primarily orally. Faith comes through hearing (cf. Rom 10:17).

Many Bible passages contain implicit or explicit references to other biblical passages, and are either a commentary on or an application of them. "The Bible interprets itself" is a venerable maxim that reminds us to interpret the Bible contextually.

Because the Bible is both timeless and time-conditioned, we should emulate our predecessors in conducting a dialogue between our circumstances and those of the Bible. Through this mirroring dimension of the Bible, *lectio divina* can reveal much about us as well as the biblical characters.

PRAYER PARTICULARS

 From a spiritual perspective, the key to interacting with the Bible optimally is to let the word of God judge us, that is, reveal areas and ways in which we need to grow and be transformed by God's love and truth. This should challenge and encourage rather than intimidate us, as in Jesus God has rendered a definitive judgment in our favor (cf. Jn 12:31-32), if only we ally ourselves and our sufferings with Him.

The alternative is to judge the Bible according to our criteria and agenda, and thereby invert the moral and spiritual order, or conversely, view the Bible as judging in the sense of condemnation rather than loving and salvific correction, thereby distorting its purpose (cf. Jn 3:17). As emphasized in Jesus' farewell address in John's Gospel (cf. Jn 14-17), the Holy Spirit is our advocate, in direct opposition to Satan, who accuses and harasses us in a matter befitting his name (derived from the Hebrew word for prosecuting attorney).

HUMILITY, RECEPTIVITY, AND RESPONSIBILITY

To experience God's word beneficially, we must be humble, receptive, and responsible. Humility and receptivity entail recognition of our dependence on divine providence and mercy. Otherwise, we'd spend all our time worrying if we are doing it right rather than simply doing our best to be present and responsive, and let the Spirit guide us. Pride obstructs God's message and our conversion. It makes us stagnant and hardened (unreceptive to God and others).

Responsibility implies that we give our best to God. The earliest biblical example is Abel, who in offering a sacrifice brought God the first fruits of his crop. This foreshadowed the Israelite law that mandated that the first fruits of the crop be offered as a sacrifice to God (cf. Ex 23:19; 34:26; Lev 2:12).

The biblical description of Cain's offering does not explicitly indicate a defect, but God's displeasure and Cain's subsequent reaction would seem to indicate that Cain's disposition was amiss. Cain's downfall reminds us that when our spiritual offerings (such as our interactions with God's word) and practical efforts do not seem fruitful, we should not resort to envy, resentment, and violence. The disparity between efforts and results has been a disconcerting mystery from the beginning (cf. Gen 3:17-19), and remains an enduring challenge not only to believers but to all persons.

As long as we are humble, receptive, and responsible in our interactions with the Bible, we can remain a work-in-progress intellectually, emotionally, and spiritually while still deriving meaning and guidance from God's word. Grace is available to us as it was to Cain, if only we will accept it (cf. Gen 4:1-8). If we are seeking ideal dispositions or circumstances, we will be disappointed. Unlike us, God does not expect perfection. Rather, he wants us to try our best and trust in Him, while avoiding complacency and presumption (spiritual arrogance, e.g., presuming upon God's mercy to excuse insincerity and wanton irresponsibility).

THE DYNAMIC EVOLUTION OF *LECTIO DIVINA*

Over the years, the Church has continued the developmental process of *lectio divina* by refining her understanding of the Bible and the way believers interact with it. In the above excerpt (pages 28-29), Pope Benedict communicated an unprecedented papal commitment to the dissemination, development, and adaptation of *lectio divina* using "carefully considered, fully up-to-date methods." This book is a response to his exhortation.

In both the Bible and life, God reveals himself and His truth gradually, according to our openness and capacity to receive it (cf. Rom 14; Heb 5:11-14). As individual believers and as a Church, our understanding of both divine and human realities is dynamic and progressive.

The early Church described their interactions with the Bible as reading and prayer. Gradually, the terms meditation and contemplation were added, although the process itself had not changed. The stage of action was initially implied, but later became explicit during the Middle Ages thanks in large part to the influence of Richard of St. Victor.

John Cassian was an influential fourth-century desert father who wrote extensively on the process of praying with and interpreting Scripture. His articulation of the various levels of meaning in the Bible is discussed in *The How-To Book of the Bible*.

In the fifth century, St. Benedict instituted daily practice of *lectio* as part of the monastic routine. Since then, *lectio* has been handed down within the Benedictine and Trappist (Cistercian) orders, and has been practiced and adapted by other religious communities. In modern times, it has again become an integral part of the spirituality of laypersons.

The post-Vatican II Church's most influential promoter of *lectio divina*, Cardinal Martini, has contributed to the evolution and adaptation of *lectio divina* by highlighting the importance of discernment, decision, and consolation, activities prominent in Jesuit spirituality. His description of such can be found in the transcript of a 1986 address on *lectio* he gave to the American bishops. It can also be found in the appendix to my book *Where Is God When You Need Him?* (Alba House).

PRAYER PASSAGES

 We live in a society superficially obsessed with wellness and potential fulfillment. Significant amounts of money are spent on attaining wellness and fulfillment at the same time that educational, entertainment, cultural, and government institutions undermine it. Conversely, the Catholic tradition reveals how to attain it for free through the exercise of the traditional virtues.

The Bible is the primary handbook on the subject. Pope Paul VI's 1967 encyclical *Populorum Progressio* (On the Development of Peoples) is the Church's most profound and far-reaching exposition of the developmental and wellness dimension of Catholicism for both individuals and communities.

Unfortunately, the Church has not adequately facilitated the application of these resources. Consequently, many believers utilize secular self-help books and programs without considering superior Christian resources.

Lectio divina is an unsurpassed resource for wellness and holistic personal growth. Throughout the book I will point out ways in which *lectio* and the Bible contribute to our wellness and fulfillment. Who can help us in these areas more than the One who made and sustains us, and fellow believers who accompany us on the journey?

THE MULTIPLE DIMENSIONS OF *LECTIO DIVINA*

Like the Bible, *lectio divina* has both a human and divine component; it involves encountering God's word as expressed in human words, and using our human faculties in cooperation with grace and the Holy Spirit.

Consequently, the Church has always defined *lectio divina* in holistic terms, consistent with the first commandment's injunction to love God with your whole self and the Bible's portrayal of the human being as a whole person. As we discuss the individual components (activities) of *lectio* in upcoming chapters, we will see how the holistic faculties (i.e., senses, mind, emotions, and spirit) are engaged and integrated naturally.

ORIGINS WITH ORIGEN: THE BIBLE IN ITS CATHOLIC CONTEXT

Origen (d. A.D. 254) was the Church's first biblical scholar and a prolific writer on the Bible. He was from the Alexandrian (Egypt) school of Christian spirituality, which emphasized the spiritual (also referred to as anagogical — pointing to God or heaven) or allegorical (i.e., symbolic, metaphorical) meaning of Scripture.

Because Origen was deeply conversant with the biblical languages and interpretive nuances of the Bible (i.e., its literal meaning), he was able to produce insightful homilies and commentaries on the Bible that have endured throughout the centuries. He was centuries before his time in advocating an inter-disciplinary approach to biblical interpretation. Anticipating modern biblical studies' incorporation of the human sciences, he taught that secular disciplines such as grammar, rhetoric, music, and geometry could contribute to a more accurate understanding of Scripture.

We can remain within orthodoxy, even though our interpretations of Scripture and Church teachings are not infallible, if we

Origen believed that all created spirits, including demons, would ultimately be saved or restored to grace, an unorthodox belief known as *apocatastasis* (Greek for "restoration") that was condemned at the Second Council of Constantinople in A.D. 553. Desiring all persons to be saved, as God does (cf. 1 Tim 2:4), is one thing; believing and proclaiming it as inevitable is another.

We can learn a sober and timely lesson from Origen. Today, when New Age and other eclectic spiritualities infiltrate grass roots Christianity, attracting believers unaware of their unorthodox implications and foundations, Origen's example reminds us that even when we sincerely and competently integrate prayer and study of the Bible, we must also avoid interpretations and applications that are opposed to the teachings of the Church.

For example, some Protestants believe in eternal security (once you accept Christ as your personal savior, you are saved irrespective of your subsequent choices and actions). This compromises free will and presumes upon God's mercy. It is an example of the distorted interpretations foreign to the mind of the biblical author that can occur when isolated Scripture texts are taken out of the context of the Bible and Catholic teaching as a whole.

---

frequently partake of prayer, the Eucharist and the Sacrament of Reconciliation, and engage in ongoing adult religious formation (spiritual and psychological development) and education (study). Opportunities for such include spiritual direction, pastoral counseling, Bible and catechism classes, faith sharing or Bible study groups, and spiritual or background reading (e.g., St. Francis de Sales' *Introduction to the Devout Life*, Thomas à Kempis' *The Imitation of Christ*, and the Catholic *Catechism of the Catholic Church*).

THE DYNAMIC NATURE OF *LECTIO DIVINA* AND THE BIBLE

Early on in our exploration we want to avoid viewing *lectio divina* as an isolated activity distinct from family, work, social, and parish life. Our goal is to make *lectio divina* an integral part of our lifestyle with implications for all aspects of our life. The primary way we do this is by bridging the message and guidance we received during our *lectio* time to the rest of our day by trying to live it and periodically returning to it as a centering point. This dynamic, interactive, contextual approach is representative of Catholic and biblical spirituality, which is inclusive and inter-related rather than compartmentalized.

The more we see the link between life and *lectio*, the more real God and the Bible will become to us. They can penetrate our conditioned, false self and bring out the person we were meant to be, thereby making us more whole and authentic.

The entire Bible was composed with an eye to life. *Lectio divina* and biblical spirituality practices evolved as cultural and ecclesiastical circumstances changed and the Church matured in its theological understanding and spiritual practices. God's word speeds on (cf. 2 Thess 3:1) and continues to be adapted according to the guidance of the Spirit and the needs of the Church.

This dynamism allows us to apply the simultaneously time-conditioned and timeless texts of the Bible to our lives in search of the meaning God has for us. Bible reading and interpretation are ultimately an exercise in balancing the Bible's literal (historical) and applied (contemporary, personal) meanings.

ACCOMMODATING THE BIBLE

Early Church fathers such as Augustine, Jerome, Ambrose, Leo the Great, and Gregory the Great wrote commentaries and gave homilies that drew out the meaning and implications of the Bible for their communities. The technical term for this is accommodation, which means accommodating the text to con-

When we pray with the Bible, we can accommodate it to our situation as long as we recognize when we are doing eisegesis (reading or projecting into the Bible our own perspective and experience for purposes of deriving personal meaning and applications) rather than exegesis (literal interpretation), and maintain these in a healthy tension so as to be faithful to both ourselves and the text.

We should not expect this synthesis to take place immediately. Prayer and study are complementary, but likewise exist in tension with each other. Finding a balance is an ongoing challenge.

For beginner purposes, we can arrive at a sufficient understanding of the literal meaning of a biblical passage through attentive reading, common sense, reasoning, utilization of basic interpretive principles such as found in this book and *The How-To Book of the Bible*, and prudent utilization of footnotes and background articles that are found in most Catholic Bibles.

Further, we do not impose our accommodated interpretation on others, nor use it to develop a personal theology distinct from Church teachings.

temporary circumstances and needs. It's as old a practice as the Bible itself, whose composition was directly responsive to the needs of its audience.

We can accommodate (adapt) not only the Bible, but *lectio divina* as well. *Lectio divina* constitutes the natural way human beings interact with God and His Word, primarily in the Bible, but also in life and through other spiritual stimuli (e.g., the Eucharist, the Sacrament of Reconciliation, the Rosary, Stations of the Cross, the writings of the Church Fathers, magisterial documents, spiritual classics, and journaling — our written response to God's word and providential initiative in our lives). The aforementioned are rooted in Scripture, and thus are innate applications of *lectio divina*.

Once you learn the objectives, activities, and flow of *lectio*, you will increasingly recognize varied opportunities for utilizing it, both planned and spontaneous, and it will become a way of life as well as a process, constituting the journey of a lifetime.

THE FLUID AND SPONTANEOUS NATURE OF *LECTIO DIVINA*

In this book I refer to *lectio divina* as a process, activity, or model, but never a method. I don't want to give the impression of something rigid or programmatic. Interactions with other human beings or God should never be viewed or experienced in a mechanical manner. You can't define or confine such interactions precisely. There has to be the spontaneity, individuality, and natural flow innate to constructive human communications and development.

However, this does not preclude principles, guidelines, pointers, and boundaries. Human beings function best with some level of guidance and structure. Human development and communications are too fragile and volatile, and human nature too vulnerable, to be approached with a carefree, "anything goes" mentality. *Lectio divina* strikes a balance between structure and spontaneity. It facilitates the dynamic, synergistic integration of inspiration (the Holy Spirit's guidance) and perspiration (human efforts).

Let us close this chapter by affirming a message particularly emphasized in the Gospels of Luke (cf. Lk 18:1-8) and John (cf. Jn 14-17), that of perseverance in prayer despite resistance. The topic is of such importance that we will devote some of the final chapter to it.

We don't practice *lectio divina* and engage the Bible primarily for enjoyment, though such may ensue as a byproduct. As in marriage, the fundamental values underlying an intimate encounter such as we experience in *lectio divina* are love and fidelity. These enable us to weather periodic experiences of boredom, discouragement, confusion, and conflict. With these realistic expectations before us, let us proceed to the individual activities of *lectio divina*.

PRAYER POSSIBILITIES

Select one or both of the following passages and consider how identification with the human circumstances of the biblical author contributes to a deeper and more personal message.

Hos 1-3: Hosea's reaction to the infidelity of Gomer, his wife, as a metaphor for God's fidelity to Israel.

- In what ways does Hosea act like a faithful but betrayed partner?
- What does Scripture's use of this imagery communicate about God and Israel and each of us?
- How is this passage's symbolism and message relevant to you?

The betrayal or disappointment you experience or perpetrate need not be confined to marriage. Biblical teachings/values have both universal/general and specific applications.

Compare the way God goes back and forth between love and anger — reflecting Hosea's emotional turbulence and thereby humanizing (the technical term being anthropomorphizing) the divine response — and your own passionate vacillation when you have been badly hurt by a loved one.

Ezek 24:15-18: God notifies Ezekiel of the impending death of his wife, "the delight of your eyes," and how his response is to be a prophetic warning to Israel.

- Who or what is the delight of your eyes?
- In what ways does that expression resonate with you?

Both God and Ezekiel say very little about the personal dimension of the event. The focus is on the prophetic significance for the people, but that does not diminish the personal meaning. Put yourself in Ezekiel's place.

- How would you feel?

- How have you felt in a similar situation?
- What emotions, experiences, and losses does the passage evoke?

Perhaps share your reaction verbally or in writing with God or Ezekiel.

Scripture often describes momentous events in a succinct, dispassionate way. It does not divulge in detail the emotions or mind-set of the characters. It wants us to fill in the blanks with details and disclosures from our lives. Accordingly, inject the specifics of your life into this passage, and engage in a dialogue with God and yourself.

Intense passages such as this are good fodder for discussion with a confessor or spiritual director. Sometimes the emotions and memories evoked by Scripture are so painful that we need help from others in bearing and working through them.

Chapter Two

———— Reading and Meditation ————

The Church does not live on herself but on the Gospel, and in the Gospel always and ever anew finds the directions for her journey. This is a point that every Christian must understand and apply to himself or herself: only those who first listen to the Word can become preachers of it. Indeed, they must not teach their own wisdom but the wisdom of God, which often appears to be foolishness in the eyes of the world (cf. 1 Corinthians 1:23).

— POPE BENEDICT XVI, ADDRESS TO THE CATHOLIC BIBLICAL FEDERATION'S INTERNATIONAL CONGRESS ON *DEI VERBUM*, SEPTEMBER 16, 2005

Reading and meditation are the first two stages in *lectio divina*. Though distinct in nature, they are so interwoven in practice that they are best discussed together.

In the early Church, no sharp distinction was made between reading and meditation. The most ancient practice of *lectio divina* within Christianity was described using only the terms reading and prayer. Meditation was considered part of reading, and contemplation was part of prayer. This reflects the seamless and interactive nature of *lectio divina*. Action, the final and synthesizing stage of *lectio divina*, was presumed until it was specifically articulated in medieval times.

In biblical times and in the early Church, meditation meant murmuring or whispering aloud and repetitively the words of the Scriptures. This was the normal way people read something they wished to internalize and memorize.

The Hebrews viewed the human person and life as a whole. Their mind was more into experience, concrete images, and tangible effects than abstraction and philosophy. Lacking means of sensate stimulation available to us today, they took in and marveled at the various dimensions of nature and persons. Their refined utilization of the senses is reflected in the perceptive and appreciative descriptions of nature found throughout the Old Testament and in Jesus' parables.

In contrast, the culturally sophisticated Greeks compartmentalized things, developing precise classifications and sharp distinctions (e.g., between body and soul). The philosophical (e.g., Socrates, Plato, Aristotle) and scientific explorations (e.g., zoology) of the Greeks necessitated such categorical thinking.

As the Church became more influenced by Greek thought and practices, it adopted some of its methodical and categorical approaches. This partly accounts for the distinctions between reading and meditation and, as we will see later, prayer and contemplation, in the literature of the desert fathers and later the monks. Originally, the process was experienced as a whole rather than broken down into distinguishable elements.

Concurrently, the Jewish tradition likewise began using more specific terminology, categories, and methodologies for their religious practices. As in Christianity, such refinements continued throughout the Middle Ages, Renaissance, and Enlightenment, and into the modern era.

These are natural, if not always smooth, evolutions for dynamic faith traditions seeking God, identity, and truth in an increasingly hostile and unbelieving world. Contemporary rediscoveries of the holistic nature of the person and the inter-related, rather than compartmentalized, nature of life are now in tension with the materialistic and utilitarian perspective of society.

We don't have precise accounts of the ancient Hebrews' methods of interacting with the Bible. Their practices were passed down orally and by example within the family, clan, and schools. Detailed descriptions came later with the development of the Talmud and rabbinical literature following the break with Christianity in the late first century.

PRAYER PARTICULARS

 Although the terms reading and meditation are familiar to us, their meaning has different nuances within the Catholic tradition. As you will see, they are fluid, interactive activities characterized by an integrated sensate and mental encounter with the text. We experience the text with our senses, reflect on it consciously, and allow it to affect us on a subconscious level through repetitive recitation and affirmation, thereby gradually healing our memories and transforming our inner messages from infantile and dysfunctional to evangelical (the good news of the Bible and Jesus) and empowering.

READING, LISTENING, AND SENSING

The first stage of *lectio divina* has traditionally been referred to by its Latin term, *lectio*, which means reading. However, the biblical peoples and their neighbors understood reading differently and more holistically than we do. Reading was an activity in which all the senses were engaged in order that the text might be taken in more fully.

When I discuss the first stage of *lectio divina* — reading — I often qualify it by appending the activities of listening and sensing. Because literacy and books were scarce, and reading was primarily done in a group setting where others could hear, listening, both with the senses and the heart, was a prominent dimension. Typically, one or more persons read aloud for the group, and then silent reflection, discussion, and prayer followed — the prototype for group practice of *lectio divina* even today (see Chapter Five).

In *lectio divina*, we utilize all of our senses when reading in order to listen to God's word with our whole selves. Other faculties (i.e., the emotional, mental, and spiritual) will become more prominent in subsequent stages of *lectio*.

THE MECHANICS OF SENSATE READING

The sensate reading that constitutes the *lectio* stage is done slowly and reflectively. There is no minimum amount of the biblical text to cover or requisite time to spend. Ideally, you will read aloud, even if in an almost imperceptible whisper to avoid disturbing others. This engages your sense of speech, hearing, and potentially taste and touch.

The medieval monks who practiced *lectio divina* spoke of tasting or savoring the words of the Bible. Reading slowly stimulates the sensation of taste. Focus and concentration bring out the depth and possibilities of the activities and relationships (i.e., with self, others, and God) of *lectio divina*. Contrast this with activities where one lacks presence and attentiveness, such as reading the newspaper while eating and being so distracted you barely taste the food.

PRAYER POINTERS

Because reading aloud is work, there may be times when you lack the energy to practice it full bore. For good reason, ancient physicians prescribed reading as exercise. Even murmuring a few words can engage your faculties on a deeper, more holistic level.

As their colorfully illuminated Bibles reveal, the medieval monks also appreciated the Bible's aesthetic and sensate dimension. Touching and viewing the Bible were part of the sacred encounter. The monks, like the rabbis, would often read by following along with their finger, which gave them a sense of touching the Word. This also slowed them and their reading down, making them more aware of grammar and vocabulary, thereby helping them discern the literal meaning of the passage. This naturally helped them enter into a comfortable pace and rhythm, thereby further disposing them to God's presence and message.

Awareness of the book in your hand further contributes to the sensate experience. Given the Bible's vivid imagery, and *lectio divina*'s slow, reflective pace, you can engage your sense of smell by transporting yourself imaginatively to the biblical scene. You can pick up the dusty odor of ancient roads and homes, the stench of farm animals, and the distinct scent of sweat under the hot sun. As you become more familiar with the Bible and its setting, this will come naturally.

Our memory and the sensate faculties operative in imaginatively recreating the biblical scene can be similarly employed when practicing *lectio* on a life experience.

DISCOVERING YOUR WORD

The procedural aspect of the reading/listening/sensing stage is simple. Once you begin reading, continue until a word, phrase, verse, or image stands out, speaks to or inspires you, or evokes some reaction. It doesn't have to be a major jolt; it is simply a subject for reflection and dialogue with God and perhaps others.

Catholic tradition refers to this as a "word" in the biblical sense of an action-oriented, energy-charged, dynamic stimulus. It can be literally just a word, but usually it is a verse(s), expression, image, memory, encounter or event.

Classic biblical expressions of the dynamism of God's word include:

- "For as the rain and the snow come down from heaven, and return not thither but water the earth, making it bring forth and sprout, giving seed to the sower and bread to the eater, so shall my word be that goes forth from my mouth; it shall not return to me empty, but it shall accomplish that which I purpose, and prosper in the thing for which I sent it" (Isa 55:10-11).

- "Is not my word like fire, says the LORD, and like a hammer which breaks the rock in pieces?" (Jer 23:29)

- "For the word of God is living and active, sharper than any two-edged sword, piercing to the division of soul and spirit, of joints and marrow, and discerning the thoughts and intentions of the heart" (Heb 4:12).

- "You have been born anew, not of perishable seed but of imperishable, through the living and abiding word of God; for 'All flesh is like grass and all its glory like the flower of grass. The grass withers, and the flower falls, but the word of the Lord abides for ever.' That word is the good news which was preached to you" (1 Pt 1: 23-25).

Sometimes your word functions just as a starter, leading you to other spiritual stimuli and messages, while at other times it remains the central point of reflection. When no word in particular stands out, use your judgment, select whatever stimulus (expression, thought, lesson, image, or memory) seems most conducive to reflection, prayer, and application, and continue your dialogue with God.

After selecting your word, slowly and rhythmically (this will come naturally in time) repeat that word, phrase, verse, or image.

This repetition ingrains the word in your consciousness and sub-consciousness, and triggers a related mental, emotional, and spiritual response in the stages of *lectio divina* that naturally follow.

If you are practicing *lectio divina* on a life experience, your word can be an aspect of nature, an interpersonal relationship or encounter, a troublesome emotion, or a significant memory. You process it roughly according to the flow and activities of the *lectio divina* model so that by bringing the stimulus and your whole self to God, you may be wholly transformed.

PRAYER POINTERS

 In the reading/listening/sensing stage, you try to experience that stimulus with as many of your senses as possible. You try to take it in and pay attention to it with your whole self, consider your reaction and what it says about you and your situation, and open yourself to any message God has for you. This sets an interactive, receptive, and holistic foundation for your experience of the rest of the *lectio divina* process.

REMINISCENCE

At times, your word will bring to mind a related experience or memory, and this becomes foremost in your consciousness. For the biblically literate, another Bible passage may come to mind. If the connection and stimulus are strong enough, this related experience, memory, or text can serve as your reflective word by itself, or in unison with the word from the passage you began with.

Medieval monks coined the term "reminiscence" to describe a biblical passage bringing to mind another passage. This is an example of how *lectio divina* engages our memory faculty. In taking us from the word at hand to a related stimulus, reminiscence serves as a natural bridge between the reading and meditation stages.

ENGAGING OUR MEMORY

Given the multitude of images projected onto us daily, and our mind's tendency to race from one stimulus to another, reminiscence should be a natural impulse and activity. It enables us to take advantage of our hyperactive energies while engaging our memory.

Reminiscence compensates in part for the loss of memorization capacity that accompanied the proliferation of written texts and in modern times other communications storage media. It exercises our memory faculty.

Reminiscence is a way of relating the biblical text to personal experiences and other biblical passages, and thereby developing a contextual, integrated, and personal understanding of God's message. It helps you experience the Bible's internal consistency and direct relevance to your life.

LINKING THE BIBLE WITH LIFE

For example, a biblical passage on betrayal would naturally bring to mind a personal experience of betrayal. A "word" from the Bible can heal or deepen our understanding of our experience and emotions, and guide us in responding appropriately. This is a positive alternative to compulsive dwelling on our difficulties and finding ourselves trapped in a stifling cycle of negativity. *Lectio divina* helps us move forward in life, rather than in a circle or reverse.

Reminiscence is an essential dimension of *lectio*, but it should not dominate the process and marginalize the biblical passage at hand. We do not want to get into the habit of flippantly foregoing the passage we are reading in favor of another one that comes to mind. We could end up bouncing all over the Bible and miss the fertile ground we started with.

Likewise, we do not want to get into the habit of impulsively abandoning the biblical passage in order to concentrate on either the cares of the day or a personal experience or memory triggered by the text. These will be there when we are done with *lectio divina*.

Of course, we can also address these as part of *lectio* by reflecting on and praying about them, then listening for the Spirit's guidance. However, we do not want to marginalize the biblical message in the process. Sometimes God's word speaks directly to our situation, so that by making it our focus we also address our temporal concerns in a natural and inspired way.

We have to exercise some degree of self-discipline and adherence to the process. If we let ourselves be distracted by each memory, emotion, or concern that springs up, we'll never experience the biblical word through which God desires to speak to us.

Conversely, if the experiences, emotions, or biblical passages brought to mind are compelling enough, we should feel free to reflect on and pray about them in the context of God's word and see where the Spirit takes us. As with most things in life and Catholicism, we want to seek out a middle ground in which we balance complementary but also potentially competing values in a healthy tension.

Ideally, we will go back and forth between the original biblical text and the associated experience, emotion, or biblical text, thereby enabling the Bible to become an inspired stimulus, sounding board, and moral criteria for our reflections. After all, the Bible is God's word in the context of our lives and the life of the Church and humanity, a personal letter designed to instruct, correct, encourage, and console (cf. 2 Tim 3:14-16).

THE PURPOSE OF MEDITATION

The meditation stage is meant to facilitate an interactive integration of the aforementioned stimuli that touch us either positively or negatively. As in a human conversation, we want to strike a balance between a free exchange of ideas and reflections and a coherent, orderly dialogue and developing theme or message. Prudent practice of *lectio divina* lies in maintaining a balance between spontaneity (e.g., reminiscence, and intuitively and reflexively going with the flow and Spirit) and self-discipline (flexible adherence to the process: focusing on the selected biblical text and repeating and reflecting upon your word).

Trust your instincts and follow the lead of the Holy Spirit. With practice, prayer, and through God's grace, you'll get a feel for "reading" the movements of the Spirit. For further guidance on discerning the Spirit's movement in your life, consult the recommended texts in the bibliography. God wishes to guide and nourish us in *lectio divina* as He does in other aspects of our lives. We are responsible participants in the process, but we are not in control.

PRAYER POINTERS

The Bible is the story of God's initiative in the world and particularly in the lives of God's people. He continues to inspire and initiate in the post-biblical age, albeit in a different manner and context. Thus when we focus on God's initiative in our life, we are in harmony with the Bible's fundamental theme.

DISTRACTIONS

One of the omnipresent issues associated with not only *lectio divina*, but also any devotional practice, is that of distractions. Very few people can sit down to read, meditate on, and pray about spiritual realities without their mind wandering. The spirit may be willing, but the flesh is weak.

In general, the simplest and most effective response to distractions is to not worry about them. Let them pass and don't give them energy. Getting upset about them and consciously trying to eliminate them only exacerbates them. In most cases, they are not worth the attention and energy, particularly when you are engaging in *lectio* and encountering God's word. If they are substantive and deserving of attention, but not urgent, you can attend to them later.

A common distraction is a new fondness or intense dislike of someone. It is natural to think about them. Denying it doesn't make the feelings go away, but expressing it in the proper time and way alleviates much of the attraction.

God can work in our lives through distractions just as He can through the word we reflect on in *lectio divina*. If a particular distraction continually surfaces, that may mean that it needs to be addressed and mitigated. It is even possible that a distraction can become our word for reflection. If the distraction is a passing annoyance, superficial thought, trivial concern, or upcoming endeavor of limited importance, it merits little expenditure of energy and attention. Try to let go of it for the moment by focusing on your word and the *lectio* process.

However, in the case of a substantive distraction such as a personal, familial, or relationship crisis or a significant decision dangling over your head, it may be beneficial to bring it to the multidimensional *lectio divina* process. This may help you arrive at some degree of resolution and peace, and then get on with your *lectio* and life.

God can manifest His presence in our lives amid both minor and major distractions. He can be found in both the details and the big picture. God always offers a positive path as an alternative to a negative one, though it may be difficult or not readily apparent at the time; you have to step out in faith, undertaking choices and actions that seem most appropriate. We can always find something positive to focus on, for example, our word or the various activities that comprise *lectio*.

We discern the importance of the distraction in order to determine our response. We can either let it go and get back to our *lectio divina* or address it through prayer and action or resolution — which is part of *lectio divina*. After addressing the distraction, we can always return to the biblical or life word that we received during *lectio divina*. The fact that *lectio divina* is not a rigid, mechanical, results-oriented, process robs distractions even further of their power.

COMING TO OUR SENSES

We often use the expression "reading people" to indicate that we sense or intuit what they're about. The sensate way we read written materials can likewise transfer to a more sensitive and appreciative experience of life in general. It begins with coming to (rediscovering) our senses, slowing down, and listening.

We often go through the day trapped in our heads, preoccupied with abstractions and compulsive thoughts, disengaged from our heart and senses and experiencing only a small part of what life has to offer.

Have you ever been preoccupied while eating a meal and hardly tasted the food? Or been so engulfed in thought while driving that you failed to notice the scenery and events around you, the subtle beauty in life that we so often take for granted? Or talked to someone while your or their mind was elsewhere? One of the benefits of getting more in touch with your senses is that you come to the present and take in more of life.

READING AND MEDITATION

As discussed above, reading and meditation originally were not identified as separate activities. They are naturally intertwined. Once ancient believers identified a biblical word that spoke to them, it was only natural to recite or murmur it repetitively. This helped them memorize and internalize it. This repetition is the original Jewish and Christian understanding of meditation.

Ps 1:2 identifies the blessed person as one who murmurs (meditates on) God's law day and night. Josh 1:8 has a similar message. The most common image of meditation in antiquity was that of rumination, a cow chewing its cud.

Because we modern folks typically are more methodical in our activities and compartmentalized in our approach to life, our transition between reading and meditation is usually more mechanical. Initially, we will have to make a conscious effort to read aloud and repetitively, since this is not instinctive in our culture.

However, through our reasoning, sensing, and intuitive capacities, and the prompting of the Spirit, with practice we will find ourselves paying attention to divine (providence) and human (significant events, encounters, perceptions, insights, and experiences) signs, integrating reading and meditation, and catalyzing our senses and memory. Reading and meditation will blend for us, as they did for our ancestors.

SUBCONSCIOUS DYNAMICS

From the early centuries of Christianity until modern times, monks have memorized the whole book of Psalms and other parts of the Bible. With so much on our minds and schedules, and so many messages and images bombarding us on a daily basis, to say nothing of our atrophied memory faculties, we have difficulty remembering a handful of passages in the Bible — but that can change.

Repetitively reciting Scripture develops our capacity for remembering and internalizing God's word. Further, when we immerse ourselves in positive stimuli such as Scripture and other spiritual literature and practices, we have less time and desire to unnecessarily expose ourselves to avoidable distractions and stifling (or worse) messages in media forums such as television, radio, the newspaper, and the movies.

Our subconscious mind works like a computer. The input and programming influences the output. With repeated exposure, God's word gradually tempers our compulsive responses, sheds light on our interior and exterior (e.g., interpersonal) struggles, and sensitizes us to the movement of the Spirit in our lives. In his presentation of *lectio*, Cardinal Martini articulates these dynamics as discernment, decision, and action.

We still have the same personality, weaknesses, and capacity for sin as before, but through the healing and transforming touch of God's word our minds and hearts become progressively susceptible to ongoing renewal and transformation (cf. Rom 12:2).

Repeated exposure to God's word can whittle away at our false self (the distortion of our personality and potential through the world's conditioning, negative experiences, and our own sinful choices) and hard-heartedness (obstinate attitudes toward God, His Word, ourselves, and our neighbor), and heal and shed light on our shadow (a Jungian term for the repressed, unconscious, and undeveloped side of the human personality and potential).

Our shadow impulses and behaviors, in layman's terms our dark side, often emerge in unpredictable times and ways, particularly when we are tired or stressed and our conscious filters are down. We experience this most frequently in intimate or family settings, where we are more apt to let down our guard and displace or project outward those internal issues we have been unable to resolve or control.

PRAYER PASSAGES

John Sanford's *Invisible Partners* (Paulist Press) illustrates the effect of the shadow on intimate relationships. Abbot Thomas Keating's book *Invitation to Life* (Element Books) describes *lectio divina's* therapeutic effects on the unconscious mind. The graces that flow from the incarnation and redemption can heal and redirect our shadow energies if we consistently open ourselves to God's word in the Bible and his initiative in our life, and respond appropriately.

DISCURSIVE MEDITATION

As part of the evolution of *lectio divina*, the practice of discursive meditation, or going from one thought to another, increased in prominence during and after the Middle Ages. Discursive meditation resembles reminiscence, except it primarily involves ideas, images, connections, and applications, rather than memories/recollections or biblical passages. In part, it grew out of the more intellectual approach to faith characteristic of the scholastic movement in theology that flourished in the thirteenth century under the influence of prominent practitioners such as Alexander of Hales, St. Albert the Great, his student St. Thomas Aquinas, and St. Bonaventure.

The scholastic theologians reintroduced ancient Greek philosophy, particularly the thought of Aristotle, into dialogue with Christian theology, and emphasized the compatibility of faith and reason. This was in part a balancing of the experiential mysticism that had characterized Eastern Christianity's spirituality in the preceding centuries.

Interestingly, after St. Thomas had a mystical encounter with God toward the end of his life, he purportedly regarded as "straw" his magnificent synthesis of Christian theology, the *Summa Theologica*, and due to illness never finished it. His experience reminds us that the personal encounter with God and the transformation that ensues as a result of *lectio divina* is more important than intellectual knowledge acquired through biblical and theological study.

The scholastic theologians' emphasis of intellectual activity did not result in *lectio divina* becoming an analytical rather than reflective process. It simply reflected *lectio's* adaptation to a change in culture and theological perspective. Providing that it is not carried to extremes, this enriches *lectio divina* by incorporating the intellectual dimension in a more integral way.

CULTURAL INFLUENCES ON *LECTIO DIVINA*

Modern persons likewise approach the Bible in a way that reflects cultural circumstances and theological and anthropological perspectives (how we view God and ourselves). We bring advanced scientific, sociological, and psychological perspectives to the Bible that are helpful for personal growth and wellness issues, though as a pragmatic, literalistic society we are much less adept at recognizing symbolic or metaphorical meanings and their applications to our lives. We are also much more prone to legalistic and fundamentalist interpretations.

An example of this deficiency would be popular interpretations of the book of Revelation that neglect its historical context and meaning and consequently engage in theologically biased and over-imaginative applications of its symbolism.

Of course, culture and society are not the primary influences on biblical spirituality and interpretation. Each person brings his or her unique background, capabilities, needs, and motivations to the Bible. Most important, we are guided by the Holy Spirit, whose timelessness transcends cultural limitations.

Discursive meditation helps you arrive at a practical application of your word by assimilating the various insights and associations the word evokes, including connections identified between biblical passages and life experiences. It can be described as inspired brainstorming, a type of spiritual reasoning and integra-

---

PRAYER PARTICULARS

 Discursive meditation helps us discover what our biblical or life word calls us to do or be, otherwise *lectio divina* can be just a head-trip or a nice spiritual feeling and emotional outlet. In discursive meditation, we use logic, reasoning, and association to make sense of the word given to us in *lectio divina*, and in conjunction with reminiscence identify parallels and connections within the Bible and to our lives.

---

tion process. We move from thought to thought with the objective of tying them together in a personal application.

Discursive meditation can be an introspective and revelatory as well as intellectual exercise. The connections you make while letting your thoughts and inspirations flow can help you get more in touch with yourself, life, others, and God.

DIFFERENT APPROACHES TO MEDITATION

Purist practitioners of *lectio divina* might object to the inclusion of discursive meditation as part of the process of *lectio divina*. They would consider it more appropriate to the practices of mental prayer or spiritual reading.

As texts became more available, the practice known as spiritual reading grew in prominence in the Middle Ages. With the Scriptures or other spiritual writings as its source material, it was designed to enlighten and motivate readers morally and spiritually, while helping them discern God's will in their lives. It was a more analytical and informative process than *lectio divina*.

A purist approach to *lectio divina*, as practiced by the traditional custodians of *lectio divina*, the Benedictines and Cistercians (Trappists), is more contemplative and includes little analysis or discursive thinking.

THE MARTINI MODEL

As mentioned in the previous chapter, renowned biblical scholar and former archbishop of Milan, Cardinal Carlo M. Martini, S.J., taught a form of *lectio divina* that reflects his Jesuit and scholarly background. The transcripts of his *lectio divina*-based presentations have been converted into numerous books, though unfortunately most are out of print.

Martini integrates critical analysis (using basic principles and methods of modern biblical studies) and practical applications of the text with *lectio*'s dialogical and contemplative dimensions, whereas the traditional, Benedictine approach is more assimilative (taking in the word through repetition and reflection and letting it resonate within us) and contemplative. There is obviously much overlap, as the process is essentially the same.

Drawing from Jesuit spirituality, Cardinal Martini emphasizes the role of discernment, decision, and consolation (the peace beyond all understanding; cf. Phil 4:7). These are implicit rather than explicitly discussed in the more traditional explanations of *lectio*. These complement the analytical and apostolic component Cardinal Martini wishes to incorporate, without de-emphasizing or subordinating the contemplative dimension.

To use the example of Lk 10:38-42, Cardinal Martini is inviting us to bring the traits of both Martha (industriousness) and Mary (contemplative receptivity) to our encounter with God's word. The suitability of his invitation varies with the circumstances and individual, so those finding this approach too

---

PRAYER PARTICULARS

When done outside of *lectio divina* so as not to impinge on its contemplative dimension, Bible study and background reading is helpful for developing the skill and knowledge base necessary for subsequently identifying the literal meaning of the biblical text as part of the *lectio* process. Competent interpretation is an essential dimension of the *lectio* process.

The objectives of spiritual reading and Bible study are different from, though complementary to, those of *lectio divina*. *Lectio divina* fosters a personal encounter with God that hopefully transforms us and bears fruit in our actions. Bible study helps us interpret and understand God's word more accurately, and spiritual reading guides and motivates us in living it. Of course, there is overlap in their objectives, activities, and results, as the spiritual life and human development are a continuum.

analytical and intense should not hesitate to stick with the traditional contemplative Benedictine approach.

It is important to distinguish *lectio divina* not only from spiritual reading but also from Bible study. Analyzing a biblical passage through critical reasoning and discursive meditation as part of the *lectio* process is different from reflexively relying on biblical commentaries and protracted analysis. The latter can be a mentally exhausting deterrent from the prayerful and contemplative aspects of *lectio divina*.

PERSONALIZED *LECTIO DIVINA* LESSONS

Some years ago I had the opportunity to sit down with one of the world's foremost monastic authorities on *lectio divina*, a Benedictine who traveled the world teaching it to other monks. I told him that I had difficulty with the contemplative aspect of *lectio divina* because my mind was active and my body restless. I had trouble slowing down my mind and sitting still once I developed personal applications from my chosen word and shared my response with God. I therefore didn't practice *lectio divina* in the textbook manner.

Utilizing Cardinal Martini's model, I approached *lectio* more analytically (using both discursive meditation and the insights of modern biblical studies), apostolically (seeking guidance in discipleship and Christian ministry), and motivationally (seeking psychological, moral, and spiritual inspiration and encouragement). I developed a customized middle ground of repetitive reading, reflection, analysis, application, prayer, and contemplation suited to my circumstances, capacities, and the movement of the Spirit.

Although this Benedictine monk taught and practiced the traditional contemplative approach, he encouraged me to practice *lectio divina* as my gifts and comfort level dictated, while staying within the broad boundaries of the model.

SUMMARY

Each person has their capabilities, preferences, and circumstances, and should feel free to respectfully and prudently personalize/customize the process of *lectio divina*. By trying the traditional principles and practices discussed in this book, you can benefit from the experience of others and the wisdom of the Church while discovering, adapting, and fine-tuning what works for you. The process is ongoing, as your needs, circumstances, and capacities change over time and the Spirit leads you "where it wills" (Jn 3:8).

In the next chapter, we will look at various applications of reading and meditation and see how these neatly transition to the next two stages of *lectio divina*, prayer and contemplation.

─────────── **PRAYER POSSIBILITIES** ───────────

Select one of the psalms, proverbs, or beatitudes and reflect on it repeatedly, so as to ingrain it in your heart and memory. Consider its application to your life and the response it calls forth from you. Recall it at different times of the day or during difficult experiences as a centering point and inspirational reminder. When you give a small portion of Scripture this type of attention, it becomes a part of you.

Chapter Three

Reading and Meditation in Context

> What does the Church recognize in Holy Scripture? It recognizes the unchangeableness of her doctrine (cf. Jn 10:35: Jesus said, "Scripture cannot be broken"). The Church recognizes the validity and permanent authenticity of God's Word contained in it; she recognizes its inexhaustible spiritual fruitfulness: she recognizes a prophetic value which can infuse with the breath of the Holy Spirit every human situation, whether it be historical or sociological; she recognizes the source of her preaching and catechesis. She particularly recognizes a spiritual nourishment.
>
> — POPE PAUL VI, JULY 1, 1970

It is important to discuss reading and meditation in practice as well as in theory. Accordingly, the following is an example of my *lectio* of a familiar text. This serves the dual purpose of relating *lectio* and the biblical text to life, as well as anticipating and previewing subsequent stages of *lectio divina*. While discussing my *lectio* experience, I will introduce and weave in various practical applications of reading and meditation, including that ever-present subject, suffering.

This chapter will serve as a bridge between *lectio* pairs (reading and meditation, prayer and contemplation) that constitute the foundational activities of our spiritual dialogue with God.

This recognizes and will exemplify their seamless continuity in the *lectio* process.

LECTIO IN ACTION

The following is an example of how I integrated an emotional, experiential, and analytical approach to a biblical passage in the context of praying with the Bible. Note how I engage in simple critical analysis (interpretive efforts) without veering into intense biblical study. Also bear in mind the subjective and abstract nature of my account, for the dynamic *lectio* process is understood better through experience than description. As Job exclaimed pursuant to his contemplative encounter with God (cf. Job 38-41), first-person experience is far more convincing than hearsay testimony (cf. Job 42:5).

LECTIO ON LOVE

> "Love is patient and kind; love is not jealous or boastful; it is not arrogant or rude. Love does not insist on its own way; it is not irritable or resentful; it does not rejoice at wrong, but rejoices in the right. Love bears all things, believes all things, hopes all things, endures all things."
>
> — 1 Cor 13:4-7

I prayerfully read 1 Cor 13, in which St. Paul describes the attributes of love. I am having a difficult time in a close relationship (sound familiar?), and decide to measure my attitude and actions against St. Paul's ideals. Instead of using the Bible and my own self-righteous defensiveness to judge and criticize others, I subject myself to the Bible's mirror-like scrutiny, trusting in God's mercy, wisdom, and support.

The text evokes intense emotions and memories, which I wrestle with in the context of St. Paul's words. I oscillate between my personal experience and perspectives and St. Paul's ideals. In a manifestation of reminiscence, other New Testament texts on love (e.g., 1 Jn 3–4) come to mind. This exemplifies the natural link between discursive meditation and reminiscence, and between the Bible and life.

Each attribute articulated by St. Paul can evoke a whole range of thoughts, memories, emotions, applications, and supplications (pleas to God for help in living up to the ideals). Rather than tackle the whole passage, I limit my reflections to 1 Cor 13:4: What does it mean to be patient, kind, unassuming, and humble in the context of my close relationship(s)? This becomes my chosen "word." I could have chosen just one attribute and had more than enough to ponder. Reading short passages and identifying a manageable "word" is a characteristic practice of *lectio divina*, for God and the Bible can say a lot with a little.

I exercise the liberty intrinsic to *lectio* and bite off as much as I feel capable of chewing at the moment. There are times when I am tired, pressed for time, or disturbed, and I am capable only of encountering a simple, concise word, which is not necessarily any less profound and enlightening than the longer ones that I typically prefer.

PRAYER PARTICULARS

 My exercise in *lectio* liberty is an example of departing from the traditional model based on personal preferences, circumstances, capacities, and the movement of the Spirit. I am doing what I am encouraging you to do: wrestle with the model and then adapt it to your needs, maintaining an ongoing awareness and at least partial application of the traditional principles and procedures so that my individuality does not marginalize the universal dimensions of the model. I want to avoid both extremes of undisciplined eclecticism (personal whim) and rigid adherence to methodology.

Typically, I gravitate toward a more comprehensive word because that is how I grew up on the Bible — studying it prayerfully rather than doing *lectio*. Some habits are difficult to relearn, and in many cases we don't need to modify them much if they work well for us and suit our capabilities. Everyone needs to experiment and refine until they discover what works for them — which can change, for the word of God and the Spirit are dynamic rather than static. It is we who choose to stagnate. They are always urging us to open ourselves further to God's grace and guidance.

As long as we stay within the broad boundaries of the model, we should feel free to personalize *lectio*, aided by prayer, discernment, and perhaps the guidance of a spiritual director or confessor. Because *lectio* is composed of such basic, flexible, and universal human activities, it leaves us a lot of room for experimentation, spontaneity, and adaptation.

It bears repeating: the key to optimal practice of *lectio* is to balance freedom and individuality with discipline and adherence to proven principles and practices. Follow the model to the extent that you can, and then improvise based on your needs and capabilities.

You and I are not so unique that we cannot substantially benefit from a model that has endured and evolved for three millennia, benefiting countless people of diverse creeds, cultures, capabilities, and circumstances. The components of *lectio* (reading, meditation, prayer, contemplation, and action) and the human faculties involved (i.e., senses, mind, emotions, and spirit) are so innate and interrelated that everyone has some experience of them.

LOOKING AHEAD: CREATIVE AND SPIRITUAL DIALOGUE

After pondering and applying the insights and directives evoked in reading and meditation, I then discuss my reflections, resolutions, and feelings with God (and with others if during a group experience of *lectio*).

If I am feeling particularly imaginative, I might engage the biblical author or protagonists (i.e., the main characters in the story) in a dialogue, and project their response. This helps me identify with them and the biblical context, which in turn brings my interpretation closer to the literal/historical level of meaning, which ultimately has to be the foundation of my Bible reading, lest I make the text say whatever I wish. In the example above, I could imaginatively dialogue with St. Paul and consider how he might respond to my particular situation, and what counsel he would offer.

Such interaction with God and the Bible, traditionally classified as the prayer stage of *lectio divina*, should in turn lead to contemplation (silent, receptive presence before the Lord).

Sharing my thoughts and feelings with St. Paul and God — or with a loved one or group members if I am practicing *lectio divina* communally — hopefully will be accompanied by receptivity to their response and feedback. Such dialogue and openness can evoke inner peace, wisdom, and humility, and make me more aware of my inner obstacles and blind spots.

After concluding the conversation and resting quietly in God's presence (the stage known as contemplation, a spiritual "cool down" after the vigorous holistic exercise undertaken in the previous stages of *lectio divina*), I then try to implement my resolutions so that my *lectio* becomes a lived experience. This constitutes the action stage.

THE THERAPEUTIC NATURE OF *LECTIO DIVINA*

Reflecting on an evocative passage such as 1 Cor 13 in the context of our relationships with loved ones may trigger challenging and even painful thoughts and memories, including reminding us of our inability to live up to the ideals. How often we fail to practice love in our closest relationships. Thank you, St. Paul, for this loving reminder!

Because it is a balanced, holistic, and gentle process, and facilitates a personal encounter with God, *lectio divina* is a great forum for processing difficult emotions and experiences. Who better to place them before than the divine healer?

My thinking becomes clearer and my emotions more manageable when I reflect on my situation in light of God's word and in the context of the Holy Spirit's inspiration. This doesn't eliminate troublesome impulses, but it does take the edge off them, and I am less likely to despair or act rashly in response to them.

My awareness that I have a process and a confidant for dealing with my troubles enables me to go on with my life activities without recycling my difficulties mentally and emotionally. *Lectio divina* is a constructive alternative to chronic worrying and griping. It helps me discover and actualize a redemptive, transformational response.

I can't prevent angry thoughts and feelings from coming into my consciousness, but I can control what I do with them. When they bombard me, I acknowledge rather than repress them, and address them with God in a frank and trusting manner. Having experienced this catharsis, I can then return with peace of mind to the biblical text in search of further divine guidance.

PRAYER POINTERS

Lectio divina can be complemented nicely by conversations with a therapist, confessor, spiritual director, or trustworthy confidant. These are constructive alternatives to continually rehashing negative emotions and experiences and letting them dominate our life and unduly influence our attitudes and actions. Addressing our troubles with God and others beats going it alone and potentially becoming stagnant, obsessed, or disillusioned.

THE FLUIDITY OF *LECTIO DIVINA*

I have previewed the next stages of *lectio divina* — prayer, contemplation, and action — because the process itself cannot be compartmentalized. There are not precise boundaries between its stages. They are fluid, interdependent, and integrated.

To distinguish among the human faculties (i.e., senses, mind, emotions, and spirit) and *lectio divina* activities/stages as precisely as I have is an oversimplification done for conceptual purposes. Obviously, all our faculties are involved in each stage, and each stage is interwoven with the others. We are simply identifying which faculty and activity typically are most operative and prominent during a given stage of the process.

We need labels and definitions in order to understand a process, but these should not make our thinking rigid and mechanical. Such descriptions cannot capture the totality and intricacies of the experience. There is no substitute for being there (direct experience).

THE INTIMATE NATURE OF *LECTIO DIVINA*

To use a parallel example and biblical metaphor, how can you adequately describe the process of human intimacy? Limiting yourself to describing the stages, objectives, and activities would make it seem mechanical and sterile, and would fail to take into account the fluid interaction and unique personal and circum-stantial variables involved. In short, its humanity would be obscured. The process is too individual and subjective to measure in words; it can be understood only through experience.

Lectio divina is a form of intimacy in that it is a highly per-sonal, meaningful, and fruitful encounter with someone you love. It is a reciprocal communication of meaning and person; in Pope John Paul II's terminology, a communion of persons. Authentic intimacy is always constituted by reciprocal self-giving rather than mutual appropriation or exploitation.

Just as intimacy has its own integrity and value independent of any pleasure or benefit derived, so *lectio divina*'s value fundamentally consists of the encounter with God, self, and others it facilitates. Like the father in the Prodigal Son story (cf. Lk 15:11-23), God actively initiates and sustains the encounter and subsequent relationship transformation in a loving and merciful fashion.

THE VARIABLE DYNAMICS OF *LECTIO DIVINA*

As with human intimacy, the dynamics of *lectio divina* vary by person and circumstance. Everyone experiences them uniquely and not necessarily consistently or uniformly. As we and our circumstances change, so does our way of relating. This is natural, since intimacy is an evolving and dynamic communication and developmental process.

Since God is a partner in the process, there is always the element of newness, surprise, mystery, and change. Every encounter with God is unique. Your experience of *lectio divina* today will differ from that of tomorrow, even if you do not perceive the differences.

As mentioned, you should not expect your experience of *lectio divina* to correspond exactly with the pattern described in these chapters. Your circumstances, inclinations, and capacities, and the mysterious and unpredictable movement of the Holy Spirit will significantly influence your experience. Knowing the general pattern experienced by believers gives you a model to follow while you adapt it to your needs.

For some people, emotions play a major role in the process, even during the typically sensate and mental activities of reading and meditation. For others, the spiritual dimension is paramount. Persons who dislike intense intellectual activity and brainstorming will likely have difficulty with discursive meditation. They may find it mentally tiring and anxiety-evoking. Others may be energized by the intellectual activity, and find the repetitive nature of rumination to be boring and even annoying. With practice, you'll develop a rhythm and approach suited to your needs.

The more familiar you become with the Bible, the more comfortable and confident you'll be, and the more you'll be able to comprehend and assimilate and relate to life. Of course, this will not take away the drudgery and dry times. As in significant relationships and endeavors, you have to take the downs with the ups and work harder once the initial novelty, infatuation, or honeymoon period wears off.

When we undergo a conversion experience and are first re-exposed to Scripture, we typically experience a temporary high that partially immunizes or blinds us to the harsh realities of the challenge we are facing and our own weaknesses and limitations. Nature and providence make things easier at first so that we do not get discouraged and fall away while our roots are not well established, like the seed lying on the path in the parable of the sower and the seed (cf. Mk 4).

PERSEVERING WITH *LECTIO DIVINA*

Rather than give up on the process when we find parts of it dry and distasteful, we can focus on the parts we are comfortable with without denying or evading the problem. By seeking and reflecting upon the roots of our difficulties, we gain greater insights into Christian truths and ourselves, particularly how we need to grow. One way that *lectio divina* facilitates wellness and potential fulfillment is by helping us to become a more self-aware and well-rounded person.

Try to attain a balance between following the process and spontaneity. Virtue is found in the middle, between freedom and self-discipline. Accordingly, do not reflexively throw out what you are initially uncomfortable with, but also don't force yourself to undertake what is unsuitable or beyond your capacities.

Develop a gradual, reflective, adaptive, trial-and-error approach to *lectio divina* as you would to an intimate relationship. Characteristics of a process or person that are difficult initially can become tolerable or even enjoyable with time. (Unfortunately, it can also work in the opposite direction, with strengths becoming weaknesses.) Our relationship with God, as with a loved one, necessitates change and adjustments.

The dynamic nature of *lectio*, human beings, and our relationship with God is such that we should expect an ongoing evolution and development that will require periodic modifications and refinements in our attitudes, behavior, and practice of *lectio*.

PRAYER POINTERS

The art of *lectio divina* is to develop your own comfort level and style, and fine-tune it as you go. Give yourself time to assimilate an approach that works for you, and don't worry about results. That's God's business. Sincere effort is all you have to worry about.

As in intimate communications, our intentions and efforts during *lectio divina* are more important than the precise mechanics of how we go about it. God will assist us, for He is the most integral part of the process.

The communications that occur as part of *lectio divina* and healthy intimate relationships are hardly conducive to quick results. Positive transformation of entrenched sins, weaknesses, and situations takes time, which is why the mode of little victories is helpful for sustaining our morale and energies.

PRAYER PONDERINGS

Are my communications with God and loved ones characterized by the dispositions cultivated within *lectio divina* (e.g., love, respect, patience, openness)?

MEDITATING ON LIFE

The above characterizations are similarly true of our response to life experiences. Our typical reaction to a significant event or encounter is to process it intellectually, emotionally, and spiritually. We reflect upon the stimulus we are processing, be it an event, encounter, emotion, or memory, until it becomes refined and entrenched in our consciousness, and hopefully leads to some application (i.e., a constructive response).

Both subconscious and conscious energies are engaged by our reflections. Our sensate and mental efforts inevitably result in an emotional, spiritual, and practical reaction, which are typically expressed in the stages identified as prayer, contemplation, and action.

Knowledge of these tendencies and dynamics gives us a grasp of how *lectio divina* fosters our spirituality, wellness, and potential fulfillment. We can then learn to channel our faculties and energies in a cohesive and purposeful fashion. As discussed above, instead of chronically recycling a painful experience/memory and the associated emotions, we can relegate them to our *lectio divina* time as a prelude or complement to wrestling with the biblical text, whereby this stimulus can come into contact with God's healing Word and presence.

In *lectio divina*, we acknowledge our wounds, needs, and dependence on God, and open ourselves to divine healing and personal transformation. In recognizing our weakness, we discover our strengths (cf. 2 Cor 12:10).

MEDITATING ON INTIMATE SUFFERING

Perhaps the best example of this is the experience of being seriously wronged by others close to us who lack remorse and perhaps even portray themselves as the victimized party. We see this frequently in broken relationships. People who denounce their (ex) partners rarely relate the whole story and their own contribution to the difficulties.

In contrast, an inspiring model for dealing with perceived betrayal is St. Joseph, who responded to Mary's pregnancy justly, quietly, and compassionately. He sought to spare her as much suffering as possible, even at the cost of sharing in that suffering himself.

Sharing our grief with others may bring relief, validation, and sympathy, but it typically does little to heal the pain of betrayal. Only by uniting our pain with Christ's and continually trying to forgive do we find meaning and some level of healing and hope. When we bring our hurt to God and His Word, we do not experience the frustrating silence, cheap validation, devil's-advocate feedback, or irritating rationalizations that we often receive from would-be comforters.

Instead, we are reminded that such shoddy treatment happened to Christ, and we can expect the same. We don't have to seek it out, pretend it is acceptable, or forego opportunities to appropriately mitigate it, but we also have to recognize it as part of the Christian's lot. Because God is just, we can confidently put our desire for justice in His hands, and invite Him to transform our heart so that we learn to forgive as we have been forgiven.

Another advantage of bringing such pain to God is that He is the Master Psychologist. He knows us and our needs better than we do, and He knows the best way for us to respond. God judges us not by condemning, but by revealing and challenging, inviting us to be better persons and rise above pettiness and resentment.

Addressing these issues in prayer or *lectio divina* does not necessarily resolve them immediately or even lessen the pain. In this world we will never derive a satisfactory understanding of tragedies or injustices. Typically, we experience insights, meaning, and consolations only partially and gradually.

The message of the New Testament, and the Beatitudes in particular, the centerpiece of Christ's moral teaching, is that we have to endure and view such suffering in light of the message and redemptive mission of Jesus (cf. Col 1:24), and courageously entrust ourselves and our circumstances to God in hope-filled anticipation of total healing and reconciliation in the next life. We can only fully address such mysteries with God in eternity.

GOD'S WORD IN LIFE

God's initiative is not limited to the Bible. He continues to be active and communicate himself in the world, and in the life of the Church and the individual, particularly those who are open to Him. Most manifestations of divine providence and communications are subtle rather than extraordinary, and require an open, humble heart to be discerned. At the cave at Mt. Horeb, where Elijah took refuge out of fear for his life, God revealed himself not through natural phenomena, the way the pagans intuited their gods speaking, but through a "still, small voice" (cf. 1 Kings 19:9-13).

Lectio divina is a forum for discerning that voice, not only in our quiet time, but as we bridge *lectio* to life through the medium of the word we receive and our corresponding applications. Our word becomes a centering point of spiritual consciousness: we return to it for strength and guidance periodically that day and henceforth when it comes to mind. Little victories (see chapter five) are a good modus operandi in the context of *lectio* because they orient us toward manageable constructive responses.

The broad Catholic understanding of God's word expands the utility and applicability of *lectio*. Using the model of *lectio*, we can process our discerned experience of God's word as revealed in nature, providential life events, the sacraments, and particularly in the vulnerable human person with whom Christ particularly identifies (cf. Mt 25:31-46), including ourselves.

The great twentieth-century psychiatrist Carl Jung wrote a famous essay on this passage, in which he pointed out that Christians rarely associate Christ with themselves when they are vulnerable and suffering. He is perceived as "out there" or in our neighbor rather than within us as well. Were we to recognize Christ's intimate presence amid our trials, we could experience meaning and consolation that would help us cope and persevere.

THE ONGOING NATURE OF *LECTIO*

The fruits and applicability of *lectio* do not end with the conclusion of our quiet time. Through the workings of the Holy Spirit, a biblical passage (particularly one you have recently reflected upon, and therefore is in your immediate consciousness) can come to mind in response to a life situation, and trigger a (perhaps abbreviated or partial, for practical reasons, but substantive nonetheless) recurrence of the *lectio* process within us. Then we find ourselves integrating responsive reflection on life and the Bible, which go together. Christianity is an incarnational religion, meaning that it is lived "in the flesh."

Discovery of the Bible's and God's direct connection to our life can trigger a deeper, more real and personal interaction, and make our experience of *lectio divina* more practical and passionate. The objective of *lectio divina* is to encounter God and His Word, and respond receptively and obediently (cf. Mt 7:21-27).

When this multi-dimensional and holistic encounter occurs, we find ourselves more integrated and whole in all aspects of our life, with fewer imbalances and dichotomies between what we profess and practice.

Whether our *lectio divina* stimulus is a word from Scripture, life, the life of the Church (i.e., the liturgy, the sacraments, devotions, Christian service and fellowship), or some combination, it is sure to engage our emotions and spirit, thereby leading to the next two stages of *lectio divina*, prayer and contemplation. We discuss them together because they are part of the same dialogue, even more so than reading and meditation. Separating prayer and contemplation would be like breaking up communications and portraying them as sequential rather than interactive.

REVIEW

Since we're halfway through the process, let's have a quick review and preview. In the reading stage, you read a short section of material from the Bible or other prime spiritual literature, such as the writings of the Church Fathers and the saints, or the Bible-permeated speeches and documents of the magisterium, and then select a word that touches you. Conditions and (your) energy level permitting, you murmur, whisper, or say aloud this stimulus repetitively so that it becomes a part of you. Tasting the word by reading aloud (at whatever volume you choose) and being sensitive to the touch of the written word makes for a

In *lectio divina*, we reciprocally offer ourselves to God, and when applicable, others (e.g., in a group or spiritual-direction setting), as part of the communication process.

As discussed in the next chapter, we consecrate (i.e., dedicate, offer) ourselves to God when we pray with the Bible, just as we offer ourselves to Jesus during the eucharistic consecration in response to His offering of himself to us.

We give ourselves to God by trying to discern and carry out His will, particularly by loving and serving our neighbor. While the primary meaning of consecration is the dedication of something special or sacred, it often includes the objective of transformation, as in *lectio divina* and the Eucharist.

fuller sensate experience, which is good preparation for the complementary holistic activities that follow.

With practice, you'll read and meditate more fluidly and rhythmically, and more easily relate what you read to what you feel, believe, and experience, which in turn will make your attitudes and actions more fluid, authentic (less conditioned), and cohesive. You'll find yourself flowing better with God, life, others, and nature as well.

Of course, such harmony does not necessarily make life easier. To the contrary, the closer we get to God, the more we see our defects and how far we need to go, and the more God challenges us. This is the experience of those called by God in the Bible (e.g., Moses, David, Jeremiah, Job, St. Peter, St. Paul) and the saints down through the ages. Like a loving parent (cf. Heb 12:5-7), God wants what is best for us, which is union with Him and our brothers and sisters. We can attain this only by being purged of selfishness and pride, a painful process that can continue even into the next life (i.e., purgatory).

In response to life experiences, we learn to observe, sense, reflect, reason, discern, internalize, assimilate, and identify parallels, connections, and applications — each of the aforementioned being an aspect of meditation — rather than react obtusely and impulsively. With practice and perseverance (nothing good comes easy!), this engages our emotions, spirit, and will in a natural and rhythmic progression, thereby leading to prayer, contemplation, and action.

Of course, this progression need not be linear. Typically, we oscillate back and forth between the stages in a unique fashion befitting our individuality and circumstances.

Though secondary to our spiritual and moral objectives, the wellness and potential fulfillment benefits of *lectio* are obvious, particularly in tandem with quality Christian resources on the subject that are readily available (see the bibliography). We have the potential fulfillment handbook (the Bible), master (God), and "expert in humanity" (the Church, in the words of Pope Paul VI) at our disposal, and fellow travelers (believers) to help and accompany us on the way.

The meditation stage of *lectio divina* is an integration of repetitive recitation, reminiscence, discursive thinking, or feeling (one emotion that is triggered by your word can lead to others), and a resolution to bring the Bible to life through some personal application or little victory. These activities are fluid and interrelated, and together evoke parallels and connections not only with other biblical texts, but also with personal insights, emotions, and experiences. We then bring these and ourselves into dialogue with God in the stages of prayer and contemplation.

These interrelated aspects of meditation actualize our various mental faculties. Repetition and reminiscence catalyzes our memory and subconscious mind, and discursive meditation utilizes our reasoning and creative capacities to help us formulate practical applications. This builds on the sensate activity in the reading stage to deepen our holistic experience and prepare us for the emotional and spiritual dimensions that ensue in the forth-coming stages of prayer and contemplation, the subjects of our next chapter.

PRAYER POSSIBILITIES

In the previous chapter, we took a brief passage from Scripture and gave it focused attention and energy. Expanding upon this practice, let's reflect on 1 Cor 13, which I discussed briefly above.

Go through St. Paul's description of love line-by-line, and consider how each of the attributes applies to your life.

- What situations, experiences or relationships are brought to mind by each?
- How does each attribute invite you to grow?
- What attitudinal, behavioral, or lifestyle modifications does it call forth?
- How might you improve your relationship with yourself and others by taking each attribute to heart and living them more fully?

Chapter Four

——— Prayer and Contemplation ———

Prayer and contemplation are among the most natural of human activities. They are complementary aspects of dialogue and intimacy with God. Perhaps the simplest way to describe them is as mutual self-disclosure.

At the risk of over-simplification, prayer is the active dimension, while contemplation is the receptive dimension. Of course, such characterizations are imprecise, as we can understand communication with God best by experience and analogy (e.g., comparison with marriage).

To make the activities of prayer and contemplation even less intimidating, remember that you have already experienced them, so you're not encountering anything new. The purpose of this chapter is to help you get back to these activities and discuss their basic principles and practices in relation to *lectio divina*.

INTEGRATED RATHER THAN SEPARATE BUT EQUAL

In most books on *lectio*, prayer and contemplation are discussed in separate chapters. There is much to say about both of them, and though they are integrally connected, they have distinct characteristics.

However, by discussing them in one chapter, we acknowledge their fluidity and complementarily. We avoid making an artificial distinction between interdependent activities.

During prayer and contemplation, we naturally oscillate between active and receptive communications, that is, speaking and listening. We tell God how we feel, present ourselves quietly to Him with an open heart, and then respond spontaneously as the Spirit moves us.

This integrated approach resembles early Church practice, where the two (like reading and meditation) were considered one. They are two sides of the same coin: the active and receptive dimensions of an encounter with God, a holy and holistic (whole person) conversation.

KEEP IT SIMPLE

Exploring prayer and contemplation together keeps our discussion succinct. Particularly for persons new to *lectio divina*, it is counterproductive to explain prayer and contemplation in great detail. The danger is that you will think that you have to follow guidelines precisely and robotically in order to engage in prayer

A prayer that epitomizes the gift of self we make in not only prayer and contemplation, but the whole of *lectio divina*, is described in "The Contemplation for Obtaining Love" section of the spiritual exercises of St. Ignatius:

> "Take and receive, O Lord, all my liberty, my memory, my understanding and all my will; all that I have and all that I possess. All this you have given me, Lord, and I return them to You. Everything is Yours; dispense them according to Your good pleasure. Grant me Your love; give me Your grace, and this is enough for me."

and contemplation properly. These are natural, instinctive activities that are better experienced than described.

The essence of prayer and contemplation is being and disclosing yourself while disposing yourself to God's response in return, and letting it happen rather than trying to control or force things according to rigid expectations and agenda. Go with the flow of the Spirit within the flexible structure of the *lectio divina* process.

Enough preliminaries; let's explore both activities individually and as an integrated experience. I will also briefly mention the preceding and following stages so that you can experience it in context.

PRAYER

After I read and reflect upon God's word and ponder its application to my life, I convey my reaction to God.

If I am upset, I do not mince or muzzle my words. If I am confused or discouraged, I let God know. If I am physically and emotionally stressed, I might shake my fist at God or engage in some other gesture of release. Remember, *lectio* is an activity of the whole person, so that when I share with God, I offer my whole self.

There are times in a close relationship when you need to express yourself in a visceral manner. Jesus did so during the agony in the garden and on the cross. He's been there, He understands. God can handle it. He's got a thick skin.

The ancient Hebrews reflected upon and communicated every aspect of their life and relationship with God. They didn't hold anything back, thereby setting an example for us. Three Old Testament books, the Psalms, Jeremiah, and Job, are particularly helpful inspirations to candid prayer. We'll briefly consider them below.

THE PSALMS

The Psalms capture the essence of prayer so well that the early Church did not include a book of prayers in the New Testament. Various types of prayer are represented in the Psalms: liturgical, penitential (confession of sin), petition, praise and thanksgiving, lament, cursing, and exhortation (i.e., the wisdom psalms, which teach us how to live). See chapter four of *The How-To Book of the Bible* for a list of psalms according to classification.

In response to various circumstances and for balance purposes (so that our spirituality does not become one-dimensional or stale), each of these forms has a place in our prayer as part of *lectio divina*.

PRAYER PONDERINGS

- What individual psalms or classifications are currently most relevant to your life?
- To what feelings, experiences, or circumstances do they apply?
- How might they help you dialogue with God about the essential issues in your life?

Not surprisingly, given human nature and the prevalence of the "why?" question that accompanies suffering, laments are the most common classification of psalms. If you are struggling and want to express this to God, the lament psalms can provide inspiration. You can use them as a starting point and change their details to fit your circumstances.

Sharing our feelings, needs, and concerns with God enables us to avoid unhealthy repression, see our situation and ourselves more clearly, and tap into the source of our strength and deliverance.

JEREMIAH AND JOB

Jeremiah and Job contain graphic laments that equal or exceed the passionate expression found in the lament psalms. Because they are concrete rather than abstract, they are easy to visualize and relate to our situation. The confessions (i.e., laments) of Jeremiah (cf. Jer 11:18-12:6; 15:10-21; 17:14-18; 18:18-23; 20:7-18) and the speeches of Job invite us to express ourselves honestly with God, even when it isn't pleasant. They validate our inclination to bring our frustrations and darkest emotions to God in hopes of guidance, healing, and transformation.

PRAYER PONDERINGS

- Am I willing to bring my pain to God through prayerful lament rather than gripe incessantly and become embittered?
- What happens when I pray my complaints rather than feel sorry for myself or take out my anger on others or myself?
- What are the crosses in my life over which I lament?
- In what ways is the Lord inviting me to peace and joy amid my trials/difficulties?

BIBLICAL AIDS TO PRAYER

Jesus provides the ultimate guidance on prayer. His example and teachings are particularly found in the Gospels of Luke and

John, and in the Sermon on the Mount (cf. Mt 5-7; Lk 6), where we find the Lord's Prayer. In the Agony in the Garden, Jesus puts the Lord's Prayer into action by submitting to God's will amid His suffering.

The Lord's Prayer's straightforward and balanced (it addresses our relationship with God, self, and neighbor) suc-cinctness is a model for the way we ought to pray during *lectio*: Neither mince nor multiply words, nor grapple for the perfect expression. As Jesus points out, God knows our needs before we express them (cf. Mt 6:8). Just share what is going on around and within you.

I typically begin my *lectio* session with a psalm. Because the Bible says a lot with a little, I don't feel constrained to read the entire psalm. One or a few lines may be enough to inspire and nourish my prayer. Those who read from the lectionary cycle or the Liturgy of the Hours encounter the Psalms along with com-

---

PRAYER PONDERINGS

The Lord's Prayer can be the subject of our *lectio* at any time, and particularly when our prayer and experience of the Bible is dry. Each petition contains a wealth of possi-bilities for prayer, reflection, and application. The Lord's Prayer is a staple that we can return to again and again, and even incorporate as part of every *lectio* session by beginning or ending with it, along with a Hail Mary and Glory Be if we wish.

Likewise, the Rosary can be recited according to the process of *lectio divina*:

- Say the prayers repetitively, slowly, and aloud if possible.
- Meditate on the sacred mysteries and consider their application to your life; what do these events have to do with your life?
- Share with God your feelings or reactions to the mysteries in the context of your life, and listen and rest in simple presence.
- Respond to the message God has for you.

plementary biblical passages. The footnotes and introduction to the Psalms in The New American Bible and The New Jerusalem Bible can help you get started, recognize the classification and context (if known) of the individual psalms, and make sense of confusing passages.

JOURNALING WITH *LECTIO DIVINA*

During prayer, I tell God and perhaps others (if I am sharing *lectio divina* in a group or with loved ones) how I feel and what the particular biblical text or my *lectio divina* word means to me. I can also record it in my journal. Journaling can be a stimulant and companion to prayer and contemplation.

The Bible contains written communications from God to us. In our journal, we write back. Journaling as part of *lectio divina* is a form of spiritual correspondence, primarily with God, but also with ourselves, loved ones, biblical characters, and others.

Journaling with *lectio divina* is a straightforward process. Typically, a journal would include some combination of the following:

- The word (portion of the biblical text) that speaks to you, and why.
- The emotions, questions, concerns, life parallels and applications, related biblical texts (i.e., reminiscence, see chapter two), and personal memories it evokes.
- Insights and lessons you derive.
- The response that the Word and Spirit evokes in you, including resolutions, actions, or attitude adjustments you feel called to undertake.

My book *Journaling with Moses and Job* provides guidance and practical examples of journaling with Scripture and life experiences using the model of *lectio divina*. It also contains an article by Scripture scholar Abbot Jerome Kodell, O.S.B., on the *lectio divina* journals compiled by medieval monks and their relevance to today.

THE DIVINE INITIATIVE

God's loving initiative is one of the fundamental themes of the Bible and our lives. I conclude my daily journal entries by identifying instances and ways in which I perceived God's initiative and presence today, recently, or in a discernible pattern over a period of time.

God's initiative will not always be readily apparent. Depending on my state of mind and heart, circumstances, and divine providence, it can take a while for me to become sufficiently perceptive and receptive. I am not looking for sensational experiences, but subtle ways in both positive and negative circumstances that God seems to be speaking and reaching out to me.

At times, hindsight is necessary in discerning God's initiative in our lives. As exemplified and noted frequently in the Old Testament and New Testament, God can be in our midst without our being aware of it (cf. Gen 18:1-15; 28:16; 1 Sam 3:1-7; Lk 24:13-16).

We may not recognize or understand what God is saying or doing at the time, but later on, perhaps during prayer, *lectio divina*, quiet time, Mass, confession, devotions, conversations with other Christians, or simply as we go about living our lives, some thought, circumstance, or event makes God's providence, presence, and call more apparent and clear.

My typical journal entry includes routine experiences, such as reaching out to others, coping with difficulties, making progress in an area of weakness, lessons learned and discoveries made, and doing good or persevering despite difficulties at home or work.

Though I rarely experience or record anything spectacular or extraordinary, I perceive God's initiative in all aspects of my life, especially those areas of sin, weakness, or hurt that seem to be getting the better of me and in which God seems least present. I not only am encouraged by but also experience St. Paul's marvelous affirmation: where sin increased, grace abounded even more (cf. Rom 5:20).

Recognition of God's initiative is a matter of faith and hope rather than concrete evidence. We walk by faith rather than by sight (cf. 2 Cor 5:7). I rely on the Holy Spirit's and Church's guidance in my discernment.

PRAYER PONDERINGS

- How might it benefit me to identify mentally or in writing perceived manifestations of God's initiative in my life?
- Am I willing to ask myself, wrestle with, pray about, and perhaps journal on the following question: "How was God in my life today?"

CONTEMPLATION

After I share my feelings with God, I become quiet and bask in His presence. I am present to God, and dispose myself to receive what He is and has for me. As revealed in the aforementioned story (cf. 1 Kings 19:11-13) of the fleeing Elijah who encounters God at the cave in silence rather than through natural phenomena, God most often speaks in the silence of our hearts and in life events and encounters if only we will dispose ourselves to pay attention and receive him.

As articulated in Brother Lawrence's classic "The Practice of the Presence of God", a traditional term for the desired disposition in this stage is simple presence. During contemplation we are particularly conscious of and responsive to our call to just "be" in the presence of God and await His Word/response.

In the preceding stages of *lectio divina* we are more active. In contemplation, the dispositions of receiving, being, and listening are most prominent. Of course, these dispositions are operative throughout the *lectio* process. Contemplation is their synthesis and culmination.

DIVINE SIGNS

The Greek word translated as contemplation, *theoria*, means "seeing." The best biblical example of contemplation as practiced within *lectio* is the theophany (a manifestation of God's presence) in Job 38-41 and Job's response in Job 40:3-5; 42:1-6.

After lamenting his situation and venting his feelings, Job becomes quiet before the Lord and experiences His presence in a special way. As he states, his faith is no longer dependent on hearsay (cf. Job 42:5).

Hearing and learning about God from others is important, but there is no substitute for personal encounters through prayer, contemplation, and divine signs (i.e., manifestations of God's initiative in life).

Scripture speaks in veiled language when narrating Job's divine encounter and those of Moses, St. Peter, St. Paul, and the Old Testament patriarchs and prophets. Personal experiences of God and His initiative cannot be precisely described. They are too transcendent and subjective (dependent on the person and circumstances).

To be authentic, divine signs must be morally consistent with God's communication of himself in the life of the Church (i.e., the Bible, Tradition, magisterial teaching, the sacraments, family and community life, and Christian service and fellowship).

Otherwise, by substituting our bias and agenda for biblical and Catholic discernment principles, we could identify almost anything as a divine sign. Discernment resources are listed in the bibliography.

CONSOLATION: DIVINE SIGNS DURING CONTEMPLATION

Barring extraordinary revelations to saints, mystics, and those chosen by God, divine signs or encounters are not normally manifested in the sensate realm in an obvious manner (i.e., where you experience God directly with your senses).

Typically, the divine sign experienced during contemplation is the peace beyond understanding spoken of by St. Paul (cf. Phil 4:7), a gift of the Spirit that spiritual writers refer to as consolation.

Personally, I have never had a sensate experience of God's presence and communications during contemplation. However, I normally experience a calming and enduring sense of inner peace (consolation), even when on the physical and emotional level I am anxious and stressed.

Contemplation does not make your problems go away. It is not designed primarily for wellness or stress management, though it can have benefits in these areas. It may not even quell troublesome emotions. It works mainly on the spiritual level to slow and calm us down, put our lives in perspective, and dispose us to God's wise and consoling influence.

This is the contemplation stage. Be still, listen, and receive.

— PRAYER PONDERINGS —

- In what situations have I experienced consolation?
- How would I describe the experience and its effect on me?

THE CHALLENGE OF CONTEMPLATION

The docile receptivity characteristic of the contemplation stage is by far the most challenging aspect of *lectio divina* for Westerners. We are conditioned to activity; it's difficult for us to sit still. In the contemplation stage, our motto is, "Don't impulsively do something, just be there with God" (cf. Ex 14:14; Ps 46:10).

I confess to being among the most restless of natives. My experience of contemplation is dominated by distractions, racing thoughts, nervous energy, and frustration over seemingly being unable to relax.

What do I do in response? Nothing! I discipline myself to sit there for a few minutes regardless of whether I seem to be benefiting from it. When I feel I've had enough, I get up and get on with my activities.

While I seemingly may not experience consolation or other spiritual, psychological, or physiological benefits from a particular quiet time, I know that my willingness to be present to God pleases Him, particularly when it is difficult for me and tantalizing alternatives beckon.

Though my hyperactive tendencies remain, over time I have become much more comfortable sitting still for a few moments. My breathing, like my meditative reading, becomes rhythmic and reminds me of its divine source. Time slows down as I "waste" time with the Lord.

Through the grace of God and my commitment to contemplation, my high-energy personality and lifestyle gradually "tone down" to the point where I increasingly enjoy not only my contemplative inactivity, but also my leisure time. I'm learning to relax and smell the roses along with the dung (cf. Job 2:8). Like the rest of *lectio*, contemplation has become a habit and respite I look forward to. If despite my restlessness I find contemplative silence to be beneficial, I am confident that you will, too.

Just a few quiet minutes with God can make a difference. With practice, you'll become more comfortable lingering with the Lord, and your time in and benefits from contemplation will increase naturally.

COOLING DOWN

It is tempting to marginalize the contemplation stage because we are fidgety, eager to get on with our busy schedule, and discouraged at God's seeming lack of response. Given that *lectio* is a spiritual exercise, contemplation is the cool-down stage necessary for a healthy, well-rounded experience. We let our sensate, mental, and spiritual faculties relax and regenerate after the

---

PRAYER PONDERINGS

- Am I willing to slow down and just be with the Lord, as I would with friends or loved ones, communicating who I am and accepting their gifts of self in return without trying to control them or the process?
- In my circumstances, what is a good setting (time and place) for this?
- Do I accept that God is pleased with my presence whether I experience Him as present (consolation) or absent (desolation)?
- What are the obstacles to my consistently spending time with the Lord? How might I overcome them?

exertions of the previous stages. It provides a transition to and spiritual reservoir for the ultimate objective of *lectio divina*: acting upon the word of God (cf. Mt 7:21-27).

Our culturally conditioned, pragmatic expectation of an immediately gratifying experience of God is not the primary goal of contemplation. Consolation is a grace that comes at God's initiative rather than ours. Our role is to be humbly and responsibly receptive to it.

The essence of contemplation is simple presence, just being with someone we love independent of the results we experience. Presence is a primary way we express our love. Words can be superfluous between lovers. Consolation goes beyond words in constituting the peace that the world cannot give (cf. Jn 14:27; 16:33).

CONTEMPLATION IS CONSECRATION

The greatest gift we can give is ourselves. God's greatest gift is himself and as created in His image, each of us. We respond to God's gift by being present receptively, as articulated by the psalmist: "Be still, and know that I am God!" (Ps 46:10) Interestingly, this verse has a military context, and its first part is sometimes translated "Stop fighting." This reminds us that even during times of conflict we are called to simple presence before the Lord.

Contemplation involves consecrating (offering) ourselves to God. The essence of covenantal love on both the divine and human (i.e., marriage) plane is giving ourselves fully to our part-

---

PRAYER PONDERINGS

- In what ways am I holding back on God?
- How might I give myself more fully?
- When I make a concerted effort to offer myself to God and others, to give my all, how is my prayer, contemplation, and life affected?

---

ner. When we "hold back," trust, communication, and intimacy break down.

THE EUCHARISTIC CONNECTION

The concept of consecration is another link between the bread of the Word (the Bible) and of the table (the Eucharist). Just as we offer ourselves with Jesus in the eucharistic commemoration of His sacrifice on the cross, so we offer ourselves to God in receptivity to His Word. We do this in the silence of contemplation and through service to neighbor as part of the consummating action stage.

Because of its liturgical, eucharistic, and community dimension, the ultimate context for *lectio divina* is the Mass. The Bible is full of divine signs, the liturgy recalls, proclaims, and celebrates them, and the Eucharist helps us encounter Jesus in them, particularly the ultimate divine signs, the cross, empty tomb, and the person and enduring presence of Jesus.

The most sacramental Gospel, John, uses the term "signs" to designate Jesus' miraculous manifestation of God's initiative in human affairs, including the multiplication of the loaves and fishes in the chapter (Jn 6) that contains John's teachings on the Eucharist, the so-called "bread of life" discourse.

When we share the Bible and Eucharist, we achieve a natural (through heightened concentration, awareness, and fellow-

---

PRAYER PONDERINGS

- During Mass, do I pay close attention to the readings proclaimed in the Liturgy of the Word and consciously offer myself to God to be transformed by the bread of the Word and the table?
- Do I believe that God is present in His Word and the Eucharist, and that I in turn must be present to my brothers and sisters through consecratory service that is the essence of eucharistic (cf. Jn 13:1-17, 34-35) spirituality?

---

ship) and spiritual (Jesus' nourishing, uniting, and healing presence among us) synergy while reminding ourselves that love of God must be complemented by love of neighbor. John highlights Jesus' washing of the apostles' feet at the Last Supper in order to identify consecratory (i.e., sanctified, self-giving) service as the essence of eucharistic spirituality. As Jesus has done, so must we do (cf. Jn 13:15, 34). The term consecratory is apt because it conveys the sacred, gratuitous, and celebratory nature of the outreach to which we are called.

PRAYER AND CONTEMPLATION IN CONTEXT

The reading and meditation stages provide the spiritual substance and inspiration that gives our dialogue with God context, structure, and direction. Otherwise, our prayer would be open-ended and subjective, that is, driven primarily by our emotions and circumstances without the guiding influence of God's word.

Such "free-form" prayer has its place in Catholic spirituality. In many contexts, it is the typical way we pray. Further, within

---

PRAYER PASSAGES

 Continuity is a fundamental attribute of *lectio divina*. The components of *lectio divina* have complementary, synergistic effects, as attested in this frequently cited quotation from *The Ladder of Monks*, by Guigo II, a twelfth-century Carthusian monk famous for his writings on *lectio divina* and contemplative spirituality:

"... reading without meditation is sterile, meditation without reading is liable to error, prayer without meditation is lukewarm, meditation without prayer is unfruitful, prayer when it is fervent wins contemplation, but to obtain it without prayer would be rare, even miraculous. However, there is no limit to God's power, and His merciful love surpasses all His other works."

---

the context of *lectio divina* we can share whatever we want with God; there are no rigid requirements that prayer and contemplation must conform to. They do not always need to be directly inspired by God's word. Our life experiences and circumstances in conjunction with the movement of the Spirit within us can also evoke prayer and contemplation.

Nonetheless, our typical practice of prayer and contemplation within *lectio divina* is to respond to the word we received during reading and meditation, share our reaction with God, and await His response in the quiet of our heart and subsequently in life events and encounters (i.e., human and divine signs). The dialogue continues as the Word is played out in life.

WRESTLING WITH THE WORD

Among the most illustrative Old Testament images of prayer are Jacob and Job wrestling with God (cf. Gen 32:24-30; Job 3-31). God does not wrestle with us in order to defeat us, but rather to engage us on a more intimate level. Analogously, married couples often find their most passionate and revelatory moments occur after they have wrestled with each other and come to a reconciliation or resolution.

God's word evokes a reaction in us. We instinctively express our feelings, hopes, fears, and needs in response to God's call. We go beyond surface feelings and encounter the essence of our emotions, experiences, and disposition. In the context of God's word and the Spirit's influence, prayer is our opportunity to share and discover who we are and how we are doing.

Contemplation is quiet time set aside to pay attention to God. We let His Word, initiative (providential events and encounters in our life), and presence resonate in the silence of our heart. We bask in His presence, submitting ourselves in humble, receptive silence, while trusting in His wisdom and mercy.

Developing a relationship with God is a never-ending process. Like Job (cf. Job 27:2-5), persist in your integrity and sincerity. Tell God what you experience, think, need, and feel, and make sure to listen for His response — let Him get a word in edgewise.

God preferred Job's passionate candor to his friends' superficial God-talk (cf. Job 42:7, 9). When we pray, God wants us to be and share ourselves. He can work with our immaturity, weaknesses, and misguided notions, but He can do little with insincerity.

PRAYER PONDERINGS

- Am I honest with God and myself in prayer, or do I suppress hurts and raw emotions?
- What happens when I relate to God in an open, trusting fashion?

BEING NATURAL WITH GOD

I have fastidiously avoided referring to *lectio divina* as a method because I don't want it to seem mechanical. You've engaged in the activities of *lectio* before, even though you might not have been conscious of the terminology, concepts, and flow. As I share highlights of what the Church has experienced and learned over the centuries about the prayer and contemplation dialogue, try to relate it to your experience of both spiritual and interpersonal communications. And remember, I am offering guidelines rather than a blueprint.

SUMMARY

Prayer and contemplation is conversation from the heart even more intimate than conversation with a loved one, as with God we need hold nothing back out of fear of hurting or angering Him. We need not factor in sensitivities and measure our words. He can handle whatever we dish out. This is liberating, consoling, and therapeutic.

Don't think about prayer and contemplation as much as do it. Particularly when starting out, don't worry about methods or techniques of prayer and contemplation. They have their usefulness, but not when we are familiarizing ourselves with *lectio*. Better to just share with God how you feel about the word you received in reading and meditation in the context of your life, and listen for the movement of the Spirit in your heart.

Above all, don't worry about doing prayer and contemplation "properly" — whatever that means. Sharing and listening/receiving sincerely are the fundamental purpose of prayer and contemplation. Prepare by doing your homework (such as reading this or other books on the topic, and perhaps attending a class or getting instructions from a spiritual director), then trust your capacities and instincts and "dance with the Spirit," that is, try to discern and follow the divine flow (i.e., where God seems to be leading you).

Spiritual communications require self-discipline and perseverance, but should not be forced or strained. Thankfully, the Spirit intercedes for us when we do not know how to pray (cf. Rom 8:26). Recognizing our poverty in prayer, and that it is the Spirit that sustains our prayer, is an important step in communicating openly with God.

If I express my feelings to God in prayer, my interior silence is enhanced and I am less inclined to inappropriately speak out and subject others to raw emotions and displaced reactions. I am also less likely to suppress my emotions and become susceptible to a personality disorder or a physical manifestation such as an ulcer or high blood pressure.

The sensate, mental, and subconscious energies evoked in reading and meditation bear expression. We need the emotional and spiritual outlet that prayer and contemplation provide, and the practical resolution of action.

Eventually our emotions will make their way out, so why not channel them constructively and proactively in a prayerful context in which we bring our whole selves before the Divine Therapist?

Like human conversations, our dialogue with God should be interactive and spontaneous. It's not as if we speak our piece, sit quietly before God, and then mechanically move forward. That's not normal human communications. Both parties have an ongoing opportunity for exchange (input and response).

Prayer and contemplation are a dialogical give and take, back and forth. Sometimes I don't have much to say, so I give God the floor. Other times, I have my say, then listen to God, or in biblical terms, wait on Him (cf. Ps 130:5-6).

Aided by the cathartic effects of prayer, the silent, responsive presence the Spirit cultivates in us during contemplation disposes us to carry out God's will in the consummating stage of *lectio divina*: action.

The action stage follows contemplation, just as the apostles had to come down to earth after the inspiring experience of the Transfiguration (cf. Mt 17:1-8). Like the Israelites as Pharaoh's army is about to overtake them at the Sea of Reeds, after lingering with God and His Word we must move forward with Him and do His will. God can lead us to water (spiritual growth), but we have to trust Him while enduring the waves (cf. Ex 14:15). The reflective and dialogical encounter of the first stages of *lectio* must be followed with a practical response, which we will discuss next.

Reread the opening quotation in this book that preceded the introduction. It invites us to devote more time to silence, prayer, and contemplation.

- In what ways are you excessively focused on external activities?
- How might you better cultivate a physical space, daily or periodic time for, love of, and receptivity to silence in your life?

Consider Jesus' circumstances, cultural milieu, and itinerant lifestyle, and imaginatively contemplate the role of silence, prayer, and contemplation in His life. Consider His appreciation of nature and how it contributed to His interior sensitivity and receptivity.

- How might you emulate His prayerful (in the sense of reverent awareness and responsiveness to an ongoing dialogue with God, others, and life) attitude and behavior, and the way He carved out quiet times?
- Given your circumstances, needs, and convictions, what attitude adjustments, actions, and lifestyle adjustments can you undertake? How might you make prayer a higher priority and more central activity and disposition in your life?

Chapter Five

Action: The Fruit of Biblical Spirituality

The final stage of *lectio divina*, action, is the perfect culmination of the reflective, responsive, and receptive modes of the preceding stages of *lectio divina*.

Action is not just the end of the process. It is integral to the entire experience. It is its synthesis, integrating and permeating its various stages.

As the word "activity" implies, we engage in some sort of action during each activity of *lectio divina*. The theme and value of action underlies all the activities of *lectio divina*, as they are undertaken not as ends in themselves, but to develop our relationship with God, self, and neighbor.

The action stage is where we manifest the fruit of our reflections and prayerful dialogue. It is constituted by the choices we make and the actions we undertake in response to the messages received and the resolutions undertaken during and following *lectio divina*. The action stage makes the process of *lectio divina* concrete, practical, and ongoing rather than static and abstract, and helps God's word to speed on (cf. 2 Thess 3:1).

PRAYER PASSAGES

Action is at the core of biblical spirituality. The Sermon on the Mount, which illustrates the morality required of Jesus' followers, ends by asserting that worship and hearing the word of God must be complemented by fidelity to God's will. Authentic spirituality bears fruit in action. We must live the faith (cf. Mt 7:15-27; Jas 1:21; 1 Jn 3:21-23; 4:20-21). Otherwise, we are like the hypocrites (the Greek root means actor) decried by Jesus (cf. Mt 23) and the Old Testament prophets.

THE INTERACTIVENESS OF *LECTIO DIVINA*

Because *lectio divina* is a communications activity, it is subjective, (inter)personal, and interactive. It is a dynamic, ongoing process that balances reflection, response, receptivity, and action. However, because we are discussing the stages individually and sequentially, there is a tendency to compartmentalize, mechanize, or ritualize the process.

Lectio divina is not a rigid, linear process in which we methodically progress through the stages in order, then we're finished until the next time. We typically oscillate between the various stages in *lectio divina* several times. Much of this occurs so naturally that we are not even conscious of the stages as we experience them. We just engage in *lectio* as a whole process and let the Spirit and the rhythm of the process lead us.

The traditional order of the *lectio divina* stages is descriptive of the typical progression people experience when prayerfully interacting with the Bible, but the Spirit blows where it wills (cf. Jn 3:8), and each person and *lectio divina* session is unique.

While each *lectio* session does not have to be balanced equally between the five activities, the ideal is to at least touch upon each of them. We want to avoid the extremes of consistently focusing on or excluding particular activities. For example, ancient (John Cassian), medieval (Guigo II), and modern (Cardinal Martini) authorities have pointed out the drawbacks of practicing contemplation independent of reading and meditation on the biblical text.

While God can speak to us in prayer and contemplation independent of the Bible, over the long haul we want to be spiritually, emotionally, and mentally anchored to the Bible in the context of the life and teachings of the Church. Satan is crafty, and loves to manipulate emotions and perceptions so as to distort the truth. God's word is truth, and serves as an antidote to the anti-word (Pope John Paul II's term for Satan).

The holistic nature of *lectio divina* facilitates memorization, internalization, and assimilation (integration in our life). If we recognize the relatedness and continuity of *lectio divina* with

---

PRAYER PARTICULARS

Personal Prayer

At times I go directly to prayer because something pressing is on my mind. Only after bringing my concerns to God am I able to concentrate upon the Bible passage. Another time I may be so into the Bible passage that I only pray it after extensive analysis and application. I may spend little time in contemplation because I can't slow my mind or body down sufficiently to sit still for long. In such cases I engage in whatever prayer and contemplation I feel capable of, and entrust myself to God's mercy and providence.

respect to the Bible and life experiences, we will experience our dialogue with God as dynamic and ongoing. Even when our *lectio divina* time concludes and we return to our activities, life and providence can thrust us back into the word and applications we experienced in *lectio divina*. Something brings our word to mind and we are inspired to act in accordance with the message(s) we have received and our subsequent resolutions.

Just as intimacy with a spouse is a spontaneous, unpredictable, and subjective dialogical process, so *lectio divina* is a non-choreographed dance undertaken with God in which we respect the steps but do not so confine ourselves to them that we marginalize spontaneity, intuition, and creativity.

ACTUALIZING YOUR WORD THROUGH LITTLE VICTORIES

In order to be practical as part of the action stage, I consider particular actions, attitude changes, or resolutions to undertake. I brainstorm little victories — manageable and measurable (so that I can gauge my progress) applications of the message I received.

Little victories are well suited to actualize and sustain my living of the message in the face of chaos and obstacles. A little victory is a manageable activity undertaken with a specific end or desired result in mind. It is designed to attain incremental progress rather than dramatic change. It depends little on external factors, and is largely within my control.

Little victories help me get started along the path rather than wait for perfect conditions or become intimidated by the challenge. Their measurability enables me to assess my progress and direction and determine what adjustments are needed, and derive confidence, satisfaction, and momentum from small steps forward. The incremental nature of the progress becomes an opportunity to humbly and gratefully affirm myself, others, and God for the grace of growth. For more on little victories, see my book *Personal Energy Management* (Loyola University Press).

Both *lectio divina* and little victories are humble yet powerful activities. Because *lectio divina* does not focus on a large portion of Scripture nor require you to read a predetermined amount, and it is not about trying to analyze and assimilate every aspect of the biblical passage, it is particularly amenable to the concept of little victories. In the context of *lectio divina*, a little victory is a manageable and measurable application of our word, something we can begin implementing and refining in the present. If we wait for a major application of the message we received, we may never get started.

The word we are given in *lectio divina*, humble and impotent as it may seem, can be the source of moral, spiritual, relational, and developmental little victories. Little victories provide moral(e) victories through the consolation and encouragement that accompanies their performance. You're not trying to change the world — just a little part of it, beginning with yourself.

For example, we may try to endure a stressful encounter with a loved one without saying something hurtful. We might avoid saying something negative about someone when others in the conversation are engaging in gossip and slander, or even better, exit the scene quietly as a sign of our disapproval.

The humble, manageable spirit underlying little victories is found throughout the Bible. In the Old Testament, little kindnesses by such unlikely heroes as Rahab (the prostitute of Jericho), Ruth, and the widow of Zarephath (cf. 1 Kings 17:7-24) result in abundant blessings. In the Gospels, Jesus extolled the little things done for God and others (e.g., the widow's treasury contribution, the cup of cold water, and hospitality for the guest who inconveniences us). Indeed, the last judgment parable (cf. Mt 25:31-46) highlights a compendium of manageable acts of charity.

GOD'S VARIOUS WAYS OF SPEAKING TO US

It is important to consider the broad context and ways in which the action stage unfolds. We speak of action not in a narrow, mechanical way, but as it relates to life and to the overall practice of *lectio* and Christian spirituality.

Action is pivotal for responding to God's word in its various manifestations, beginning with Jesus (cf. Jn 1; 1 Jn 1) and by adoption and association (cf. Mt 25:31-46) all human persons, particularly those who are vulnerable and suffering. Next in authority and importance comes the Eucharist and the Bible and Tradition — which Vatican II speaks of as related sources of revelation that "flow from the same divine wellspring."

God speaks to us through the sacraments, the saints, the magisterium, Christian fellowship and community, family life, life events, and nature. Each of these manifestations of God's word can inspire in us the activities of *lectio divina. Lectio* brings us closer to God, self, others, and nature through the medium of God's word.

God can speak to us through whatever channels He wishes, but the aforementioned are the most common, orthodox, and attested. Who are we to limit God? Who would anticipate that God would speak loudest and redeem the world through the crucifixion of an apparent criminal and rejected prophet?

PRAYER PARTICULARS

 As a matter of theological discretion, we should remember that when we speak of God as communicating through nature, we exclude any pantheistic notions (in which God is closely identified with nature) such as prevalent in today's New Age spiritualities and ancient polytheism. We should view nature through the lens of Gen 1-2, the psalms (e.g., Ps 8, 103, 104), the parables and teachings of Jesus in which He reveals His perceptive appreciation of nature, and other biblical texts (e.g., Isaiah, Job 38-41, Wisdom), which present nature as God's handiwork.

The broad way Catholics understand God's word is rooted in the Bible and Tradition, and is reflective of God's omnipresence and providence. It does not water down God's word, but rather recognizes and distinguishes between the different levels of authority discussed above. For example, the Bible and Tradition are normative expressions of God's word, and thus we would obviously spend more time listening to God in Scripture than in nature, without, of course, excluding the latter.

In accordance with the paradoxical and balanced nature of Catholic faith, we do not give God's written word an elevated status beyond that accorded it by Jesus and the Bible itself. Like the Sabbath, God's written word was made for humanity, rather than the reverse.

THE CONTEXTS OF THE BIBLE

The Bible must be always be understood in its canonical (all 84 books taken together), historical, communal, and ecclesiastical (the Church is both servant and guardian of the word) contexts.

PRAYER PARTICULARS

Ultimately, the Bible is more than any one of us can handle autonomously. For optimum understanding and interactions, we encounter the Bible in union with the Church at its various levels: universal, local, and familial (what Vatican Council II referred to as the domestic church).

Sharing the Bible with fellow Christians, reading books and magisterial documents and addresses that extensively reference the Bible, and most important, hearing it proclaimed at Mass are ways in which we complement and enrich our individual encounters with the Bible. These enable us to beneficially practice private reading and praying of the Bible without developing an independent, self-sufficient approach that leads to pride, misunderstanding, and division.

The synergistic and focusing effect of group brainstorming and dialogue along with the presence of the Lord (cf. Mt 18:16-17) are why St. Gregory the Great, one of the Church's most influential and insightful commentators on Scripture, pointed out that we typically get more out of the Bible when reflecting on it with others. Accordingly, at the end of this chapter is a model for group Bible sharing using the *lectio divina* model.

SILENCE AND ACTIONS SPEAK LOUDER THAN WORDS

Lectio's objective is to put us in intimate and responsive dialogue with God's word. Recalling the biblical analogy of marriage as symbolic of our relationship with God, such intimacy can be wordless and composed of presence, gestures, and actions — words do not always suffice. The contemplation stage has a wordless dimension in that we dwell silently with God and communicate through presence and desire rather than language.

The action stage functions as a corrective and preventive to hard-heartedness, which is the biblical term for obtuseness and disobedience to God's word. *Lectio divina* is designed to evoke in us a sensitivity and obedience/responsiveness to God's word. This counteracts our cultural conditioning and inner compulsion to pursue and impose our will and agenda rather than God's.

PRAYING CONSTANTLY

Because prayer and action are intertwined in life as well as in *lectio divina*, it is fitting that in our discussion of the action stage we consider the complementary and dynamic role of prayer. The message we receive in *lectio divina* can be a bridge to our day and a centering point amid our many activities. It reminds us that God and our spiritual life do not go away until we return to pray. In fact, perhaps the best way to sum up the spirit of *lectio divina* is St. Paul's oft-quoted exhortation, "pray constantly" (1 Thess 5:17).

Lest we dismiss this as simply the product of St. Paul's idealism and enthusiasm, we should recall that the Lord himself counseled us to "pray always" (Lk 18:1), and gave us a parable (the persistent widow; cf. Lk 18:1-8) to illustrate such.

Ongoing prayer is critical to the spirituality and apostolic life of the individual and the Church. It lifts *lectio divina* out of the realm of a Bible reading and prayer model and into its natural, intended status as a way of spirituality and life.

Little victories are a manageable and encouraging way of implementing the resolutions and lessons we derive when praying constantly. They enable us to maintain a healthy pace, energy level, and spiritual and emotional equilibrium as we endeavor to remain continually open to God's call and communications.

DEFINING PRAYER IN BIBLICAL TERMS

Our initial reaction to this exhortation to constant prayer is one of surprise, if not bewilderment: How can anyone pray constantly? We are flesh as well as spirit.

Who can consistently operate on that level?

These concerns reflect an overly activist understanding of prayer that overlooks the role of the Spirit. Rom 7-8 is our point of departure for understanding both our limitations and possibilities.

In Rom 7:14-25, St. Paul laments our inability to act in accordance with our best intentions: the spirit is willing, but the flesh is weak (cf. Mt 26:41). In Rom 8, St. Paul discusses how the Spirit can assume center stage if we allow it, culminating in the Spirit interceding for and praying in us amid our weakness (cf. Rom 8:26-27). Praying constantly means to walk in the Spirit mindful of the Father's love poured out in Christ Jesus. Consistent with the overall theme of the Bible, such prayer does not come at our initiative, but as a response to God's outreach.

Viewing Rom 7-8 together, we recognize the tension between the flesh and the spirit that characterizes all of life and spirituality, including *lectio*, and that there are outside forces seeking to pull us down or build us up. St. Paul's paradoxical response is that we can overcome all our obstacles, interior and external, through the redemptive love of Jesus (cf. Rom 8:31-39). Thus when we feel disappointed in our *lectio* experience we should turn to Jesus for inspiration, consolation, and guidance, trusting that He can bring good out of our situation (cf. Rom 8:28), rather than get down on ourselves or God.

THE TIMELESSNESS OF THE BIBLE

The God of the Bible is a living God whose providential initiative does not stop with the Bible. Though the canon of the Bible is closed (no new books will be added), in an existential sense it remains an open book — the essence of its events, circumstances, characters, challenges, and lessons re-occur in our lives if only we open our eyes and hearts to perceive and respond to them. The events in the Bible are timeless as well as time-conditioned (historical).

The words of the Bible are letters addressed to us individually and communally, reminding us that we assume the dual role of actors and audience. The Bible is our story, and is essential to making sense of our lives.

PRAYER PASSAGES

 Who has not seen the parable of the Good Samaritan, the widow's mite (poor people giving generously), the prodigal son, and the rich man and Lazarus re-enacted in their presence? Who has not experienced family tensions and rivalries such as recorded in the accounts of the patriarchs and matriarchs and Jewish kings, and even in God-fearing households such as Tobit and Anna's (cf. Tob 2:11-14), Job's (cf. Job 2:9-10), and the disciples of Bethany (Mary, Martha, and Lazarus)? Who has not joined the apostles and crowds in responding with bewilderment to the Lord's demands and "hard sayings" (cf. Mt 19:10; Jn 6:60-66)?

THE COOPERATIVE AND DIALOGICAL NATURE OF PRAYER

This brings us to the very heart of the nature of prayer. As described by St. Teresa of Avila, it is conversation with the One who loves us. Prayer is not what we do of ourselves; it is not an autonomous activity. We have a senior and controlling (i.e., providential) partner, God. Prayer is cooperation with the Spirit who prays within and for us.

Jesus is the vine and we are the branches. As we integrate prayer and action, God prunes us (cf. Jn 15:2) in preparation for eternity. The pain that accompanies such correction is an invitation to deeper intimacy with the Lord and fellow sufferers.

Spiritual dialogue (reading, meditation, prayer, and contemplation) and action go together. Praying with the Bible includes praying about and amid life. *Lectio divina* facilitates a dynamic Christian lifestyle whereby we recognize the integral link between the Bible and our lives and the importance of emulating Mary, the model disciple, in contemplating the word of God in our heart (cf. Lk 2:19) and obeying it by sharing in the cross and redemptive mission of Christ (cf. Jn 19:25-27; Col 1:24).

Praying constantly includes reflective recitation of prayers such as the Lord's Prayer, the Hail Mary, the Rosary, or other formal or informal prayers, but is not limited to such. Because prayer is always a response to God's initiative in our lives and the movement of the Spirit in our hearts, it cannot be narrowly defined. Prayer is grace (the gratuitous initiative of God) first, and human response second.

Through the intercession of the Spirit (cf. Rom 8:26-27), we can pray constantly even when we don't feel conscious or capable of it. When we persevere amid discouragement or desolation (the absence of God and inner peace), we can transcend our feelings and trust that God is both present and pleased with us. Jesus continually reminds us of God's concern for the wayward sheep and of His own mission to the sick more so than to the healthy.

- In what ways do I feel capable of praying constantly?
- Which prayer forms and models work well for me?
- How might I be more diligent in practicing them?
- What are the obstacles to my praying constantly?
- How do I respond when I don't feel capable of praying?
- How do I experience God in those moments?
- What might He be conveying to me amid the silence and emptiness?

THE SPIRIT VERSUS THE LETTER

The message God has for us in *lectio divina* can be implied as well as explicitly stated in Scripture. It is a movement of the heart that forms our conscience and guides our attitudes and actions.

For example, one of my deepest convictions after years of praying with the Bible and participating in the public and pastoral life of the Church is that charity must permeate our words and actions, particularly with respect to fellow Christians whom we dislike and disapprove of. I may not approve of the behavior or stance of a loved one, peer, pastor, bishop, or even pope (he's got the toughest job and therefore is most vulnerable to scrutiny and criticism), but that does not give me the right to publicly or socially vilify them.

I cringe when I hear Christians make disrespectful public comments about fellow Christians, particularly leaders or prominent persons with considerable responsibilities. Often such comments are made without sufficient knowledge of the circumstances or one's own bias and agenda. Persons under scrutiny are due the benefit of the doubt until they prove undeserving.

Both Jesus and St. Paul (cf. Mt 18; 1 Cor 6) provided guidelines for addressing wrongs and disputes within the Christian community. While such conflict-resolution forums are rarely readily available today, that still does not justify publicly degrading and humiliating others. When slander spreads and scandal occurs, everyone loses.

Even though we might not be able to reference a particular passage that articulates this principle, we know that charity in Christian relations is either implicit and presumed or explicit throughout the New Testament. In integrating, balancing, and heeding implied and literal meanings of Scripture, we are operating according to their mind-set (cf. 1 Cor 2:16), which is a desired affect of *lectio divina*.

Sometimes we discover that the Spirit touches our heart and transcends our finite knowledge. For example, there may be a biblical text that directly corresponds to our intuition, situation, or application, but we either haven't encountered it or can't remember the wording or its location in the Bible, yet we intuit its essence. Our limited familiarity with the Bible should not impede us from following the stirrings of the Spirit in our heart, providing, of course, that we do not neglect study or the literal sense of the Bible, nor embrace anything that conflicts with Church or biblical teaching.

While it is nice to be able to quote the Bible chapter and verse, it is more important to comprehend and live its message. The Spirit helps us discern and digest its message, and through frequent readings the Word gradually becomes part of us. Because we are seeking the message God has for us, rather than attempting to develop a personal theology that we will impose on others or the Church, we have considerable freedom in applying the biblical text to our situation.

Obviously, we want to remain within the bounds of the text's literal meaning, but we need not get hung up about exact correspondence of details to our life. The New Testament writers certainly didn't worry about that, for when they reference particular Old Testament passages it is obvious that they don't feel

The more we read the Bible, the more the experience of reminiscence (discussed in chapter two) — one scriptural passage or providential life experience evoking another — will come naturally to us. Eventually, the Bible will become part of our memory and vocabulary, to be recalled in the midst of life experiences through the inspiration of the Spirit.

This is how our Jewish and Christian ancestors experienced the Bible — not through academic commentaries or proof-reading arguments to determine whose interpretation is correct, but by listening to the Spirit in their hearts as individuals and as a community. The same Spirit who inspired the Bible is working within us to help us take it to heart and live it.

---

constrained to a rigidly literal rendering. They focus on the essential and applied/contemporary meaning of the original text.

For example, personal applications with regards to Martha's hyperactive fussiness (cf. Lk 10:38-42) need not be restricted to hospitality or homemaking. Rather, they can focus on the essential values in the passage, in this case losing sight of the primacy of God's word over our agenda-driven activism.

At times it will be the overall thrust of the inspired writer's message, rather than a specific verse(s), that speaks to us. It may be the underlying attitude and approach communicated by the writer, and the respect and expectations he has for the community he is writing to. His example (a life dedicated to Jesus and the Church) speaks loudest of all.

Likewise, it is our example, more so than our words, which will proclaim the good news of the Bible to others. In this spiritual rather than legalistic, overly literal approach to the Bible we epitomize the words of St. Paul: the letter kills, but the spirit gives life (cf. 2 Cor 3:6).

UTILIZING THE BIBLE PROPERLY

Lectio divina is far from a fundamentalist, proof-texting, rigid religious practice. It is as much a way of life as a process. Biblical religion boils down to love — justice, mercy, and compassion take priority over sacrifice and ritual observance (cf. Hos 6:6; Mic 6:6-8; Mt 9:13; Isa 58; Ps 50; Sir 28:1-7). Besides the homage they rightly render to God, worship and religious rituals have their greatest utility and meaning when they are linked to the way we live.

We can't expect to have a verbatim Bible quote on hand for every circumstance. A substantial aspect of the action stage is stepping out in faith. We expose ourselves to God's word in the Bible, wrestle with it, and then try to live it as best we can. God does not provide answers so much as questions.

PRAYER POINTERS

The Bible is not an answer book. It poses questions that challenge us to die to ourselves while paradoxically becoming fully ourselves and fulfilling our potential. Living the Bible often comes down to applications of love of God, self, and neighbor that transcend legalism and fundamentalistic moralism and require prudence, discernment, and self-giving/sacrifice.

Most of the Bible's moral exhortations and prescriptions are framed in general terms because precise situational applications would be both endless and inadequate. The subjectivity and nuances of each person, relationship, and circumstance mitigate against sweeping generalizations.

We need to reflect on the situations and choices before us, pray and listen for spiritual guidance, do research and seek counsel when necessary, apply common sense and the fruits of our *lectio* reflections and analysis, and identify/empathize with others in order to bring the Bible to bear correctly in particular situations.

Of course, this does not preclude receiving straightforward, concrete guidance from God's word. For example, it is not uncommon to encounter married persons in crisis situations. They may be on the brink of separation and divorce. Modern psychology, popular culture, and the legal and social system provide plenty of opportunities and rationalizations for compromising integrity and principle and entering into inappropriate interactions with the person.

Malachi (cf. Mal 2:16), Jesus, St. Paul, and the author of Hebrews (cf. Heb 13:4) make it quite clear: There is no excuse for violating the covenant of marriage and the dignity of the spouses, even when the spouses are vulnerable and behave inappropriately.

THE CENTRALITY OF ACTION

We could go on and on with examples. The main point of this chapter is that the action stage of *lectio divina* is the junction at which the Bible and life, God and ourselves, and ideals and reality come together. We either assume the role of the first son who said yes but didn't follow through or of the second son who initially resisted but turned around and did what he was asked (cf. Mt 21:28-32).

The context and metaphor of the aforementioned parable is that of working in the vineyard, a ripe analogy (pun intended!) for the process of *lectio*. Action is where we bring the word of God we receive to the vineyard of life and hopefully bear fruit — which is not necessarily the same as "successful" efforts, for God can work through both triumphs and setbacks.

Typically, the loudest we speak is through actions. Love is the ultimate prayer and act of worship. Praying always isn't limited to continuously reciting prayers or thinking about God. It means being in ongoing receptivity to God, which at times can transcend words and consciousness — through the Spirit working within us. It implies an openness to God's word constituted by listening, sharing with God and others, and obedience. The biblical refrain "do whatever he tells you" (cf. Jn 2:5; Gen 41:55; Ex 19:8; 24:3) is an example of a lived prayer and spiritual motto.

THE PERVASIVENESS OF *LECTIO DIVINA*

Because of the importance of living our faith, most of this chapter is concerned with action's synthesizing dimension; that is, how it permeates and integrates the *lectio divina* process both in our direct encounters with God's word in the Bible and in its providential manifestations in life. *Lectio divina* is an integrated, fluid process of disposing ourselves to God's word in quiet time as preparation for and in dialogue with the challenge of living it.

Sometimes we engage in *lectio divina* as a response to life encounters or events in which God's initiative (word and providence) invites us to dialogue, reflection, and repentance. As so many biblical characters discovered, from Abraham, Moses, and David to St. Peter and St. Paul, God is calling us not to our agenda and project, but to His.

Through whatever setting it occurs, be it quiet time, in nature, with others in a group or liturgical setting, or in the cauldron of life, *lectio divina* disposes us to God's word. Ultimately, *lectio divina* is both dialogue and challenge, in the words of the Bible an agonizing struggle (cf. Lk 22:44; 1 Cor 9:24-27) to prepare ourselves to share in the Gospel's blessings (cf. 1 Cor 9:23). We commune with God for strength and guidance (cf. Ex 14:13-14), but ultimately we have to move forward amid obstacles and uncertainty (cf. Ex 14:15). This is the action stage.

In the just-cited reference, even Moses is revealed as hesitant and unsure. He needed prompts from God, just as we do. God often issues these prompts not only through the Bible, but also through life, both in the secular world, where God remains active, and in the Church, through Christian community, counsel, teachings, and the sacraments. *Lectio divina* is about reading and heeding these divine and human signs, and in turn being a sign for others.

THE COMMUNAL DIMENSION OF *LECTIO DIVINA*

Because *lectio divina* is a communication process, it has an innate interpersonal component. Combined with the fact that the Bible is a community document in origin, development, and application, it is natural to practice *lectio divina* in a group context. Jesus emphatically encouraged group spirituality: "Again I say to you, if two of you agree on earth about anything they ask, it will be done for them by my Father in heaven. For where two or three are gathered in my name, there am I in the midst of them" (Mt 18:19-20).

As mentioned, hearing the Bible proclaimed in a communal setting fosters a group brainstorming effect and a sharper personal presence inspired by positive peer pressure: "Iron sharpens iron, and one man sharpens another" (Prov 27:17). Folks want to help one another, and no one wants to look bad by approaching the text sloppily, as is a temptation when we practice *lectio divina* privately.

Translating *lectio divina* to a group setting requires some adaptations, though the activities and objectives are essentially the same. There is not an exact correspondence because, since the Church's transition from an oral to a written culture and with the proliferation of books and literacy, *lectio divina* has mostly been explained and practiced as a private process.

However, as discussed in chapter one, *lectio divina's* roots are in the communal experience of an oral culture. Even today, believers who participate in small or "base" Christian communities practice a form of group *lectio divina* similar to that described below. In emulating the Bible's original oral and communal setting, we can tap into its essential values and practices in a way that will refine our individual practice as well.

GROUP *LECTIO DIVINA* MODEL

Following are general guidelines for practicing *lectio divina* in a family or group setting:

- Greet one another and allow sufficient time to acclimate yourselves to one another and to the environment.
- Begin by incorporating the communal intercession dimension recommended by Jesus (cf. Mt 18:20). Give all participants the opportunity to share something they'd like the group to pray for.
- Set the tone by beginning with a few lines from the Bible, preferably a psalm, perhaps the one used in the upcoming or previous Sunday liturgy. Either designate one person to read it or read it aloud as a group as is my preference. The latter may be awkward at first, but it instills the habit of reading aloud in a slow, rhythmic pace.
- The most common and appropriate material for group *lectio* is one or more of the Sunday readings from the lectionary. This prepares us for Mass and helps us follow-up

on the message we receive. If possible, divide the reading into at least two parts so that a member of each sex can read it. Read the passage slowly, sufficiently loud, and if appropriate, dramatically.

- During three to four minutes of quiet reflection, the participants each select and reflect on a "word" (i.e., phrase, verse, image, etc.) that touched them. The leader breaks the silence and invites the participants to share their words without explaining them.

- Since this is not an intimate revelation, most people are willing to share their word. Those uncomfortable at first generally become less hesitant once they get used to the setting and process. However, each person retains the right to keep his or her word private.

- At first, some participants will forget that during this initial exchange they are not to explain the reasons for choosing their word. When this occurs, let them talk for a few moments rather than cut them off abruptly. Then, gently remind them of the guidelines for the process.

- If feasible, different members of both sexes read the passage for the second time.

- After three to four minutes of further reflection, this time with an emphasis on practical applications of their word, the participants are given the opportunity to share (at their discretion) why they chose their word, and how they intend to apply/live it. This stimulates discussion, with an emphasis on listening.

- After each person has had a turn and time runs out, or the discussion reaches a stopping point, the group closes with a few moments of silence, prayer, and perhaps a brief reading by either an individual or the group from one of the Sunday texts or the psalm. Then it is up to everyone to live what they have received and shared.

Reading this book is itself an affirmation that the spiritual journey is not undertaken in solitude or isolation. Even habitual, professed readers of the Bible such as monks and religious come together for prayer, counsel, and fellowship. The majority of our insights into *lectio divina* come through others, either directly or indirectly, and through providential life experiences discerned in the Spirit. The word of God is a community affair above all; even our individual time with God's word must bear fruit in and be influenced by interactions with others.

In accordance with the innate community dimension of the Bible and Catholic faith, it seemed fitting to end our discussion of the *lectio divina* process with guidelines for adapting it to a group setting. Group *lectio divina* is an opportunity for us to share insights and experiences, discern God's message collectively, and in solidarity sustain our efforts to live it.

CONCLUSION

Action is the pervasive and unifying component of *lectio divina*. During the other activities, we keep in mind how the word of God is inviting us to respond. The action stage represents our commitment to live the word we received in *lectio divina* and in life according to conscience and the guidance of the Spirit and the Church — not only the magisterium, but fellow Christians, well versed in Church teaching and the Bible, who are walking in the Spirit.

In the next chapter, we will explore how to begin and continue reading the Bible in a coherent and manageable fashion. I will highlight key books and programs suitable for *lectio divina*.

The Gospels have several parables dealing with seeds. Page through the Gospels until you come across one or more of these passages that speaks to you, and reflect upon them.

- What are the seeds of God's word in your life? What message and lessons is He trying to implant in you?
- Spiritually speaking, what type of soil (cf. Mk 4:1-20) are you?
- What interior and external obstacles are keeping you from bearing fruit according to your vocation, circumstances, and capabilities?
- How might you address these — for example, through prudent, purposeful actions, reformed attitudes, silent reflection and dialogue with God and perhaps others, and personal applications of God's word?

Chapter Six

—————— Reading Plans for Praying ——————
With the Bible

> But above all, the Church's spirituality will come forth enriched and nourished by the faithful reading of Sacred Scripture, of the Holy Fathers and Doctors of the Church and by all that brings about in the Church such an awareness. We mean systematic and accurate instruction, participation in that incomparable school of words, signs and divine inspirations which constitute the Sacred Liturgy and by silent and fervent meditation on divine truths and finally by wholehearted dedication to contemplative prayer.
>
> — PAUL VI, *ECCLESIAM SUAM*, AUGUST 6, 1964

Praying with the Bible as a venue for an encounter with God (cf. Job 38-42:6) simplifies the process of selecting spiritual reading material. For Catholics, there are two formal programs for praying the Bible liturgically, that is, as an act of worship in union with others and the Church's liturgical calendar. These are particularly good for beginners because they provide structure and a seasonal and thematic progression of texts. Obscure or antiquated passages (e.g., dietary and worship regulations in Leviticus) are generally excluded, making the program accessible to persons at all levels of familiarity with the Bible.

THE LITURGY OF THE HOURS

The Liturgy of the Hours is the Church's official prayer book. Monks, priests, and religious pray it daily, and it is appropriate for laypersons as well. It contains readings from the Bible, particularly the Psalms, along with prayers, intercessions, and readings from the writings of the Church Fathers and saints.

The complete Liturgy of the Hours is a four-volume set that can be overwhelming for beginners and busy persons. *Christian Prayer* is the abridged version that contains the complete texts of Morning and Evening Prayer for the entire year.

Periodic daily prayer times are observed in Judaism and Islam as well. The Liturgy of the Hours provides prayers and Scripture readings for various times during the day (e.g., morning, midday, and evening prayer).

The Liturgy of the Hours is helpful for the structure and continuity it provides, and the communion with fellow believers attained when saying the prayers at prescribed daily intervals. Of course, for individuals praying it privately there is no need for scrupulosity. If you miss a prayer time you can always pray later and either do the missed readings and prayers or go on to the next ones. Entrust your schedule and practice to God and do the best you can.

There is also no requirement that you pray all the prescribed passages and prayers presented as a unit (e.g., Monday evening prayer, Tuesday morning prayer). Whether you use the full or abridged version, even a sampling can suffice. It is better to fol-

---

PRAYER POINTERS

If you are interested in trying the Liturgy of the Hours, probably the best way to start is by requesting a library copy or seeking a used copy. Before you make a significant investment, try it out. It is usually better to build up to the complete version. See the bibliography for resources on the Liturgy of the Hours.

low the Liturgy of the Hours format imprecisely and modify it to your capabilities and schedule rather than not try at all.

THE LECTIONARY

Another liturgical but less rigorous way of praying with the Bible is to follow the readings used on Sundays and holy days and, for the more ambitious, at daily Mass as well. The book containing these is known as the Lectionary. Pocket-sized books containing these for private use are known as missals.

The Lectionary readings require less time and commitment than the Liturgy of the Hours and enrich your participation in the Mass by facilitating greater comprehension of the readings and homily and their personal relevance. If you are unable or do not feel called to attend daily Mass, then prayerfully meditating upon the Lectionary selections is a good alternative.

The Sunday Lectionary readings are divided into a three-year cycle denominated A, B, and C. Most of the Gospel readings from year A are taken from Matthew, B from Mark (with the option of using readings from John during several consecutive weeks in "Ordinary Time"), and C from Luke. John is prominent during Lent of each year, particularly on such solemn days as Holy Thursday and Good Friday. The Lectionary's Old Testament readings and responsorial psalms typically correspond to the Gospel selection, while the readings from the New Testament epistles (letters) occasionally do.

Because good passages were inevitably left out or excessively abridged during the compilation of the Lectionary, for context purposes it is helpful to have the Bible at hand during your *lectio divina* session. The Lectionary does not contain the entire Bible, but the passages deemed most essential to the faith and the liturgical season.

For persons new to praying the Bible, following the Lectionary is probably the best way to begin. You can always try the Liturgy of the Hours if you find yourself attracted to the struc-

PRAYER POINTERS

Many parishes have instituted Small Christian Communities (Bible sharing, prayer, and fellowship groups) as a way of fostering a deeper, more intimate level of community and spirituality within the parish and the family. These are modeled after base communities in third world countries, particularly in South America, where literacy and books can be scarce. The group reads, reflects upon, prays about, and discusses the upcoming Sunday readings in the context of their lives. I highly recommend participation in these in conjunction with private *lectio divina*.

For all but the most scholarly, a Bible-sharing format is preferable to a Bible-study agenda for parish or family *lectio divina* sessions because it is more balanced and holistic and requires less structure and background. Bible studies too often become forums for speculation, intellectualizing rather than internalizing, ideologies, and preconceived opinions rather than holistic engagement and assimilation of the text. The discussion and biblical message too often stays in the head and does not reach the heart.

ture and periodic prayer times, or use a less formal approach if you are structure-averse.

LOVE AS AN ANALOGY OF THE ROLE OF TIME IN PRAYER

With either liturgical approach, you don't have to go through each or all of the readings exhaustively in one sitting, particularly because you are using the "word"-driven *lectio divina* approach that focuses on a small and manageable portion of Scripture. As discussed, *lectio divina* is spontaneous and Spirit-driven as well as disciplined, so you are neither on the clock nor bound scrupulously by format. Significant human relationships and endeavors such as praying with the Bible are stifled when subjected to rigid expectations and agendas.

Lectio divina is distinguished by its relative imperviousness to time; like lovers, we linger with God and focus on our partner and the moment rather than the constraints of time. Love and spirituality have a timelessness and liberty in the Spirit that opens us to new possibilities, including the suffering that accompanies all authentic relationships.

When lovers get together, without necessarily being aware of the terms or concepts, they innately experience their companionship in terms of being and reality — rather than philosophically (describing or categorizing it), empirically (measuring it quantitatively), or expediently/functionally (according to what is accomplished).

The same goes for our dialogue and companionship with God. It is primarily to be experienced, appreciated, and celebrated rather than described, measured, or analyzed. In both human and spiritual intimacy, we are participating in a dialogue and dance that engages us in ways and directions that cannot be anticipated or programmed, but with the Spirit as our guide we can take heart from the Bible's fundamental exhortation: Fear not.

PRAYER PONDERINGS

- What is my experience of time in prayer? Does it drag or fly by?
- With regards to *lectio divina*, do I experience time as a resource and boundary or as a constraint and impediment?
- Do I give God and my prayer life — and myself — sufficient time?

INFORMAL READING PROGRAMS

If you wish to pray with the Bible, and neither of the liturgical methods discussed above suit you, consider consulting chapter six of *The How-To Book of the Bible* for additional possibilities. It contains guidelines for determining the reading plan best suited to your needs, and it offers a variety of approaches beyond the scope of this book.

If you wish to get started right away, there is nothing wrong with simply opening up your Bible and beginning to read and pray using the *lectio divina* format/progression. Start with the New Testament and, particularly, the Gospels. You can also look up familiar Old Testament passages if you know where to find them. Sample the book of Psalms, perhaps going through it in order and reading all or a portion of a psalm each day. The responsorial psalm at Mass is an example of a partial partaking of a psalm.

The Old Testament is more challenging and requires a selective approach for beginners. The *How-To Book of the Bible* outlines the books of the Old Testament and highlights its most important and accessible passages. The advantage of the aforementioned liturgical approaches is that they make the selections for you.

Because praying with the Bible puts the accent on God's initiative and the Spirit, there is less emphasis on covering a lot of material. There is no need to rush through the passage and concern ourselves with what's next. God can speak volumes in small portions of Scripture just as in seemingly insignificant events in life. Because we are praying with the Bible in the context of our life, God's initiative in our life can also gain our attention, slowing down the process even more.

Once you get started and enter into a spiritual groove/flow, the Holy Spirit and your instincts will take over, and you will find yourself in an evolving and dynamic conversation with God. Like newlyweds who embark upon a life together, gradually you will develop familiarity with your endeavor/vocation and partner and get into a rhythm, developing personal communication (reading and prayer) patterns that will help you relate with greater receptivity, awareness, and understanding, whether to a spouse or the Bible and God.

THE PACE OF PRAYER: FORGET SPEED READING!

Numerous books offer reading plans for going through the whole Bible in a year. This is not one of them. Take your time. God is not in a hurry in dealing with us. As Archbishop Fulton J. Sheen often remarked, love is never in a hurry.

It is important to be aware of the productivity mentality that can creep into our spiritual practices. We can focus on results rather than efforts, on feelings rather than principles, and unconsciously make God simply another line on our to-do list.

There is so much in each Bible text and encounter with God that it is better to operate according to the movement of the

Spirit and at our own pace and intensity level. When I prayerfully encounter the Bible, it is wise and therapeutic for me to take my time with the Lord. I need to slow down so that I can receive the Lord and His word in His time and way, not mine.

Praying with the Bible is an appointment with God, and here I am checking my watch. Doesn't the Creator of time deserve some of mine? Any time expended can be made up when I go back to my activities, due to a combination of divine providence and the revitalized energy, attitude, and perspective I will bring.

Because it involves divine and human mysteries and engages our whole selves, the Bible is not a book to be read quickly or according to a rigid, predetermined agenda. Savor it. Wrestle with it. Be amazed and edified (spiritually uplifted) by it. Accept its benevolent and empowering challenge. When it comes off as dry, confusing, and frustrating, persevere with it as you would with a loved one. With increased familiarity with the Bible and the experience of praying with it, you will cope more effectively with such difficulties and even discover ways of deriving spiritual and developmental benefit from them.

SYNTHESIZING TIME AND PACE:
THE THREE-MINUTE RULE

For those with tight resources and schedules, a serene, deliberate pace may seem like an unattainable luxury, but spiritually it is a necessity. Time-challenged readers, meet the three-minute rule. Everyone needs at least three minutes or more with the Lord on a daily or twice-daily basis — primarily for spiritual reasons, but also for health and wellness purposes. Just as we check in with a loved one throughout the day, so we make the effort to meet our Maker and monitor what is going on inside and around us.

We all waste much more than three or six minutes daily, so we can certainly spare it for God. There is no significance associated with the number "three" other than it seems the minimum amount of time one can spend with God in one sitting on a consistent basis and still touch upon the essentials.

PATIENCE IN PRAYER

Follow-up and perseverance are necessary for all growth, but particularly for that in the spiritual and moral life. Especially when practicing *lectio divina*, praying with the Bible is a form of communication. In his first encyclical, *Ecclesiam Suam* ("Paths of the Church," August 6, 1964), which served as a spiritual charter for implementing Vatican Council II, Pope Paul VI articulated principles and practices necessary for sound communications from both a human and Christian standpoint. Among those that apply directly to *lectio divina*, the following stands out:

"Before it could be completely successful the dialogue of salvation had normally to begin in small things. It progressed gradually step by step (cf. Mt 13:31). Our dialogue too must take cognizance of the slowness of human and historical development, and wait for the hour when God may make it effective.

We should not however on that account postpone until tomorrow what we can accomplish today. We should be eager for the opportune moment and sense the preciousness of time (cf. Eph 5:16). Today, every day, should see a renewal of our dialogue" (Paul VI, *Ecclesiam Suam*, Paths of the Church, August 6, 1964).

Although Paul VI's words were addressed primarily to interactions with others, they apply equally to our relationship with God. Paul VI uses the term "dialogue of salvation," which captures the fundamental purpose of *lectio*.

Accordingly, we can expect our progress in *lectio* to be humble and gradual, dependent on both our cooperation and grace. We need to pray or practice *lectio* daily, and respond enthusiastically to the divine initiative.

The three-minute rule is a good yardstick, not only for beginners, but for those who habitually pray and read the Bible extensively during their quiet time with the Lord, but increasingly recognize the need to adopt the Liturgy of the Hours principle of periodic check-ins with the Lord during the day for purposes of centering and re-focusing on God's word and initiative.

CONCLUSION

As mentioned throughout this book and the Bible, the best analogy for our relationship with God is marriage. Communication is essential to our relationship with God and our loved ones.

As in friendship and marriage, once we develop a proper framework for understanding and relating to the Bible in its context, we are better prepared to respond to its mysteries and challenges. This we have undertaken in the previous chapters, but the educational process is ongoing. As St. Augustine observed, the more he encountered the Bible the more he realized how little he knew.

Marriage, prayer, and the Bible are like a mirror in which we come face-to-face with ourselves and our partner, and discover more deeply who we are. They also expose us to a range of emotions and experiences that we may be neither prepared nor inclined to face.

We will not always like or understand what we encounter in our human or divine partner. We are tempted to deny, fight, or avoid it. What doesn't fit our agenda we seek to rationalize, remold, or discard.

Perseverance in communications is essential for sustaining our relationship with God and our loved ones. In the next chapter, we will explore how this can deepen and stabilize our experience of praying with the Bible, and enable us to bear fruits in God's time.

PRAYER POSSIBILITIES

Compose your own Bible-reading plan, or acknowledge in writing (thereby holding yourself accountable) which of the ones discussed in this chapter you are inclined to pursue. Don't feel locked into your first choice. Try it, give it a reasonable amount of time, and modify your approach as necessary. Our needs, circumstances, and inclinations as well as the movement and call of the Spirit are not static; as we and life change, so should our methods.

Jot down your hopes, objectives, and concerns, and your sense of the direction the Spirit is leading you with respect to praying with the Bible. Your goals, expectations, intentions, and plans need not be lofty, elaborate, precise, or set in stone. Make a starting point, and refine as you go along. Reread this later to see how you've grown and evolved.

Putting your plan in writing forces you to think concretely about your Bible-reading direction and activities. It also fosters a more open (less inhibited) dialogue with God, and a more objective consideration of our own capacities, motives, behavior, and needs.

Consider making this entry in a journal, perhaps as the start of a *lectio divina* journal in which you record the following:

- What you experience in life and prayer.

- How you feel about God, His word, presence (or absence), and providence/initiative in your life.
- The insights, corrections, consolations, and exhortations you receive from Scripture and fellow believers.

Chapter Seven

—————— The Art and Vocation of ——————
Persevering With the Bible

> The Holy Spirit, who has led the chosen people by inspiring the authors of the Sacred Scriptures, opens the hearts of believers to understand their meaning. This same Spirit is actively present in the Eucharistic celebration when the priest, "in persona Christi," says the words of consecration, changing the bread and wine into the Body and Blood of Christ for the spiritual nourishment of the faithful. In order to progress on our earthly pilgrimage toward the heavenly Kingdom, we all need to be nourished by the Word and the bread of eternal Life, and these are inseparable from one another!
>
> — POPE BENEDICT XVI, MESSAGE TO THE YOUTHS OF THE WORLD ON WORLD YOUTH DAY, APRIL 9, 2006

PERSEVERING WITH THE BIBLE

Giving its stabilizing influence in the Bible and life and on our practice of *lectio divina*, it is fitting to conclude this book on the subject of perseverance. *Lectio divina* is not only a process, but a lifestyle and vocation based on a relationship. Our human experiences testify to the inherent difficulties associated with such. God's central role will only make it more mysterious and less subject to our control. To sustain the practice of *lectio divina*, you must endure dry, confusing, frustrating, and even disheartening times.

Perseverance is as important in our relationship with God as it is with our loved ones. The first quality St. Paul uses to describe love in 1 Cor 13 is patience, a parallel virtue to perseverance. The Bible verse (cf. Jas 5:11) that gave rise to the expression "the patience of Job" more precisely refers to perseverance, as reflected in most modern translations.

Anyone can be momentarily inspired and instructed by the Bible. This is akin to romantic infatuation — not bad in itself, and necessary initially as part of the process of forming a bond, but it is not an end in itself. Persevering when God (or your partner) seems absent or arbitrary and your efforts seem fruitless is an authentic sign of love and fidelity.

LIVING THE BIBLE IN THE REAL WORLD

You may not feel or realize it, but you become even closer to Jesus, the Bible, the saints, and fellow Christians during tough times, for you are following the path blazed by many biblical characters, particularly Jesus, who underwent similar trials.

Analogously, spouses or family members who persevere amid trials eventually find their love and understanding deepened. So many of our earthly institutions and experiences, particularly fundamental ones such as marriage and family, are mirrored in spiritual truths and realities.

As Dietrich Bonhoeffer, the Lutheran theologian who was convicted of treason and imprisoned and executed by the Nazis, pointed out in a letter written from prison the day after a failed assassination attempt against Hitler, it is precisely by immersing ourselves fully in life while entrusting ourselves to God that we come to mature faith. *Lectio divina* is a tool for maintaining a dynamic dialogue with God in the real world of our individual and collective lives.

The Bible promises blissful existence only in reference to heaven. Earthly experiences of peace and joy are inevitably accompanied by sorrow and trials (cf. Jn 16:20, 33). *Lectio* does not enable us to bypass or minimize these difficulties, but to draw strength and guidance from God in the midst of them. *Lectio divina* helps us discover that the essential challenges of biblical events, characters, teachings, and circumstances are repeated in our lives, and sheds light on their meaning, particularly with respect to experiences of suffering and sin. It offers a graced forum for dialogue with God and the accompanying healing and transformation.

PERSEVERING TO THE END

The importance of final perseverance is illustrated dramatically in the death of Jesus. Each of the Gospels ends with Jesus uttering words indicative of His fidelity. In Luke, he quotes Ps 31:5 in committing himself fully and finally to the Lord. In John, He proclaims that His mission is completed, and then hands over the Spirit. Matthew and Mark record words that surprise or even scandalize us at first, but on further reflection we discover their appropriateness and profound personal and universal relevance. We will consider them now.

While undergoing excruciating, unrepeatable suffering, Jesus asks God the most human of questions, "Why?" The self-giving love and authenticity that accompany His plea distinguish it and serve as an example for us.

Jesus' love for God and us is revealed most strikingly when all seems lost and His desolation reaches its peak in His last moments. He does not abandon us or His heavenly father. Such fidelity is also the objective of marriage. The two central characteristics of God in the Old Testament, *hesed* (loving kindness associated with covenantal relationships) and *'emet* (fidelity) capture this devotion. In the prologue of John (cf. Jn 1:14-17) we meet their New Testament synonyms, grace and truth.

A PERSONAL EXAMPLE OF *LECTIO DIVINA*

I recently prayed with this text in light of difficult life experiences. In reflecting upon my failures and disappointments, I felt resentment toward God and others. This obviously influenced my interaction with the Scriptures and made the experience particularly dry and laborious, even aggravating. There are down days with God and the Bible just as in human relationships.

My abiding feeling was, "What's the point? I've had enough. Get someone else to do your dirty work." In considering my attitude, I recognized some biblical precedents and connections.

Moses was initially hesitant to accept God's invitation to lead Israel (cf. Ex 4:1-13), and subsequently bemoaned his and Israel's plight on several occasions (cf. Ex 17:1-4; Num 20:2-13). Jeremiah frequently lamented his vocation (see the so-called confessions of Jeremiah, cf. Jer 11:18-12:17; 15:5-21; 17:1-18; 18:18-23; 20:7-18), but the Hound of Heaven (to borrow Francis Thompson's poetic expression) isn't that easily dissuaded. Thankfully, the Lord is persistent and long-suffering with each of us.

Despite my discomfort, I stayed with the dialogue, lingering with the Lord in silence. In the language of the Psalms, I waited on the Lord. Then, in a pattern often described in the Psalms (cf. Ps 22, 73, 77), the Holy Spirit penetrated my obtuseness and remedied the accompanying fatigue, hurt, and defenses. Like the prodigal son (cf. Lk 15:17) I came to my senses, got my second wind, and entered into a deeper relationship with God, His word, and myself.

CONSIDERING THE PERSON

In my dryness I used my imagination and senses to hear Jesus' cry and draw parallels and applications to my life. To use the expression and spirituality of St. Ignatius, I "considered (i.e., reflected upon, related to, identified with) the person," in this case, Jesus.

In pondering Jesus' stark cry, I recognized parallels to my feelings and experiences. Though my circumstances are not as dire, I feel similarly at times. I am comforted that He is there with me, offering redemptive possibilities that flow from His death and resurrection. In an important passage frequently referenced by Pope Paul VI, Pope John Paul II, and Pope Benedict XVI, St. Paul observes that when we accept Christ's sufferings, which "overflow" to us (cf. 2 Cor 1:5), they become redemptive: they build up the Church and contribute to the salvation of the world (cf. Col 1:24).

Not just intellectual recognition, but also faith assent, fraternal support, and internalization of the redemptive potential of suffering make it more tolerable. Knowing that Jesus and countless brothers and sisters in the faith suffer in union with me helps me persevere, even when my circumstances do not improve or even worsen.

Faith does not necessarily lessen suffering; it gives it meaning, purpose, and direction, turning us toward God and others in fidelity to the redemptive mission we participate in and the ways our brothers and sisters and God need us. It takes our mind off ourselves and to an extent, our pain, and focuses us on our Christian vocation, in particular God's personal will/plan for us. I believe such recognition helped Jesus endure His pain, for He was human like us. In prayer, I wrestle with this belief and my hope before God, and listen for His response.

I recognized that Jesus was willing to experience unimaginable suffering so that we could know the depth of His love and presence, no matter how dire the circumstances. This pitiful cry of a broken man was not, as evangelists Luke and John brought out through the more hopeful dying words of Jesus in their Gospels, a sign of despair, but of total giving, obedience, and identification with both humanity and God the Father.

JESUS DIED AS HE LIVED

As Pope Paul VI pointed out in a 1964 address to disabled persons, our capacity for love is equivalent to our capacity for suffering. Jesus' death was consistent with what He preached and lived, offering the ultimate gift of self out of love for humanity and obedience to His Father's mysterious will. His death was the culmination of the total sharing of the human experience and the revelation of the Father that was His life.

Jesus' final moments were an immersion into the most painful and fundamental human experience, that of perceived alienation from God. I derive great comfort from knowing that Jesus can be found in my experience of alienation and abandonment, which He has redeemed and infused with divine love, truth, and presence. As evidenced throughout the Gospels and as highlighted in this passage and the parable of the last judgment (cf. Mt 25:31-46), Jesus is truly Emmanuel, God with us (cf. Mt 1:23; 18:19-20), and we are called to manifest this truth, love, and presence to others.

LIFE PARALLELS TO THE BIBLE

As illustrated in the above reflection, as you persevere in your prayerful dialogue with God you will observe the continuity between God's word/initiative in the Bible and in life, and thereby experience divine revelation as dynamic and personal rather than static and abstract.

You will discover personal parallels and connections to biblical characters, events, circumstances, and teachings that can serve as practical and inspirational signposts in your life. The message we receive from the Bible and providence (God's initiative in our life) function as divine signs (the Gospel of John's term for miracles and Jesus' revelation of His identity) in the context of human "signs of the times" (cf. Mt 16:3; a signature expression of Vatican Council II that calls us to respond prudently and evangelically [in the spirit of the Gospel] to the world around us.) They can help us discern God's will and how we need to respond and grow.

In contrast to the pagan religions of Jesus' time and the New Age and materialistic philosophies of our day, the Bible reveals a personal God who is directly involved in our life and desirous of maintaining a dialogue and personal relationship with us.

DISCERNIBLE PATTERNS IN THE TIMING OF GOD'S INITIATIVE

When praying with the Bible, I have found that breakthrough growth and discoveries most frequently occur when I am discouraged and need a lift. This pattern is often illustrated in the Bible. God seems to defer rescuing individuals and the community until they have hit bottom or are on the verge of disaster. Like the angel calling out to Abraham to desist from carrying out the sacrifice of Isaac, God seems to operate in a "last minute Charlie" manner. Perhaps He is inviting our trust, openness, and obedience in the face of suffering and uncertainty. This can reveal both the depth of our faith and areas in which we need to grow.

Fruitful praying with the Bible requires that I am consistently open to viewing and responding to the biblical text and my life in a new way, approaching them with hope, openness, and resolve. No matter how discouraged I become, I must never presume that God and the Bible have nothing more to say to me, and that I can't grow and heal. I never know what God and life have in store for me. Each encounter with God and the Bible has possibilities beyond my imagination, if only I am open to receiving them.

SUMMARY AND REVIEW
- Praying with the Bible includes other activities naturally associated with the Bible and with which we are familiar: reading, reflecting, interpreting, relating (deriving personal parallels and applications), and responding.
- The fundamental dynamic that gives meaning and direction to the experience of *lectio divina* is God's initiative in the Bible and our lives. We are always respondents

rather than initiators. Grace precedes and empowers our intentions and efforts (cf. Rom 5:8; 1 Jn 4:19).

- Praying with a biblical passage means not only pondering and interpreting it (determining its literal/historical meaning as the foundation for your personal application and prayer), but also discussing it with God, and when appropriate, others, in the context of your life, asking for help in applying and living it, and in the silence of contemplation (simple presence before the Lord) listening receptively and responsively.

- Praying with the Bible is a natural and intuitive as well as a learned and cultivated experience. It is an art and discipline rather than a science, in that it cannot be quantified or programmed and ultimately transcends description. Like the Bible itself, it is concrete rather than abstract. In order to be even partially comprehended, it must be experienced — hence the extended example above.

PRAYER PASSAGES

 There are many ways and stimulants of prayer. The Bible is an essential one because it is God's word and presence in a definitive way. May we pray and wrestle with it perseveringly as we continually discover its relevance to our life:

"Blessed is the man who walks not in the counsel of the wicked, nor stands in the way of sinners, nor sits in the seat of scoffers; but his delight is in the law of the Lord, and on his law he meditates day and night. He is like a tree planted by streams of water, that yields its fruit in its season, and its leaf does not wither. In all that he does, he prospers." (Ps 1:1-3)

- Practice and familiarity are necessary for the improvement of any relationship or endeavor. Gradually, many of the texts that seem strange and intimidating will become less so. We will progressively recognize the profound truths and personal relevance of the Bible, along with the hard-heartedness (resistance to God's word and repentance) that obstructs our peace, growth, and fulfillment.

CONCLUSION

In this chapter, I overviewed and provided a personal example of the practice of praying with the Bible. Perhaps it evoked parallels with your own perspectives and experiences, and inspired you to think about your own approach to praying with the Bible. Having engaged in detailed discussion of *lectio divina* in previous chapters, I wanted to exemplify the personal and universal issues involved (e.g., the "Why?" response to suffering).

While it is helpful to learn terminology, principles, and practices handed down within the Church, through the guidance of the Spirit, practice, and an open heart we can also learn much on our own. Information and formation (experience) can be complementary. Our dialogue with God must be free and personal as well as disciplined and structured. Even a process as natural, flexible, and spontaneous as *lectio divina* can be a deterrent to prayer when practiced in a rigid or mechanical manner.

So, prepare for a challenging adventure. Take your time and soak in the experience. Rest in the peace of a present Lord. As articulated in this chapter's opening quotation, the Church acknowledges the real presence of the Lord in the Eucharist, God's word, and Christian fellowship, so as Jesus reminded His apostles both before (cf. Jn 14:27, 16:33) and after His passion (cf. Jn 20:19, 21, 26), we should be at peace and fear not.

"Fear Not!" was a signature expression of John Paul II throughout his papacy, and for good reason: "I have said this to you, that in me you may have peace. In the world you have tribulation; but be of good cheer, I have overcome the world" (Jn 16:33).

POSTSCRIPT

This chapter was originally the first chapter of the book. In the seemingly endless cycle of revising the manuscript, I was continually reminded that the ongoing and cyclical nature of *lectio divina* and our dialogue with God is such that we often end where we begin, and vice-versa. We keep coming back to basics and central truths that we never quite grasp or master. Interestingly, I had to make very few changes in order to convert this chapter from a beginning to an ending.

The cohesive structure of the Gospel of John and the Bible as a whole is instructive in this regard. John prefaces his Gospel and the public ministry of Jesus (and to a lesser extent his first letter) with a preparatory and synthesizing prologue, and the Gospels similarly precede Jesus' passion (in John's theology, His glorification) with a preview of coming events (cf. Jn 14-17; Mt 24; Mk 13; Lk 21). Like the Gospel of John (cf. Gen 1:1; Jn 1:1),

---

PRAYER PONDERINGS

- Am I willing to pray with the Bible each time as if it is my first and last time?
- Am I willing to love others, particularly those close to me and fellow believers, as if I was encountering them for the first and last time?

As I go through my day, and attempt to apply the message I received during my prayer time, may I endeavor to keep in mind the inseparable link between love of God, self, and neighbor, and the prayerful essence of love/charity — when I reach out to others, my actions become a prayer most pleasing to God, because the person I ultimately serve is Jesus — in human disguise (cf. Isa 53; Mt 25:31-46).

---

the final book of the Bible, Revelation, contains numerous references to the first book of the Bible, Genesis, and concludes with a reference to the tree of life and a warning about the consequences of rejecting God's word (cf. Rev 22:18-19; Gen 2:9, 15-17), which recalls God's initial instruction to Adam.

In many ways the Bible, and even individual biblical books, bring us full circle. Life is like this as well. We often end up back where we began, wiser and humbler, perhaps, but nonetheless called to take up our cross anew and continue along the way the Lord is leading us. Life, human relationships, and spirituality continually invite us to start over, as exemplified most explicitly in the fundamental value of forgiveness.

As we struggle to be obedient to God's word/initiative in the Bible and in our lives, let us prayerfully begin and end with Jesus, keeping our sights fixed on Him (cf. Heb 12:1-2) as He comes to us not only in the Eucharist, sacraments, and Bible, but in the unfolding events of our lives, and most especially in the person of ourselves and our neighbor in need (cf. Mt 25:31-46).

PRAYER POSSIBILITIES

One of the common threads in the Bible, the Church, and each of our lives is God's initiative. "We love, because he first loved us" (1 Jn 4:19).

As you read through the Bible, be alert for examples of God's (the Old Testament), Jesus' (in the Gospels), and the Spirit's (Acts of the Apostles, the Epistles, and our lives) initiative.

- How is God speaking to that person, family, or community, and what applications can you make to your own life?
- What parallels can you identify between your experiences and circumstances and those of other believers, past or present, individual or collective?

These are the types of questions you want to ponder as you reflect on the Scriptures. These are spiritual exercises designed to help you discover the personal dimension of the Bible and divine providence.

- Consider ending your prayer or spiritual journaling time with a reflection on or articulation of your perception of God's initiative in your life, your sense of the Spirit's movement in your heart, and the response you discern God is asking of you.
- Consider the ways you cooperate with or resist God's initiative, and bring this in prayer to the Lord. In both our prayer and active life, we need a balance of encouragement, consolation, and correction. We should not expect or cultivate non-stop affirmation, exultation, or fault-finding, whether with respect to God, ourselves, or others.

Bibliography

General Works on the Bible

Boadt, Lawrence. *Reading the Old Testament: An Introduction.* Mahwah, N.J.: Paulist Press, 1985.

Brown, Raymond E. *An Introduction to the New Testament.* New York: Doubleday, 1997. (Reference work for intermediate and advanced readers.)

———. *Responses to 101 Questions on the Bible.* Mahwah, N.J.: Paulist Press, 1990.

Brown, Raymond E., Fitzmyer, Joseph A., and Murphy, Roland E. (editors). *The New Jerome Biblical Commentary.* New York: Prentice Hall, Inc. 1990. The best one-volume Catholic commentary. The original JBC, though dated (1968), remains useful.

Burt, Donald X. The *Pilgrim God: A Preacher Reflects on the Story of Jesus.* Collegeville, Minn.: The Liturgical Press, 1995. (Prayerful reflections on the Bible by a gifted writer.)

Charpentier, Etienne. *How to Read the Bible.* New York: Gramercy Books, 1991.

Dumm, Demetrius. *Flowers in the Desert: A Spirituality of the Bible.* Petersham, Mass.: St. Bede's Publications, 1998.

Guardini, Romano. *The Lord.* Chicago: Regnery Gateway, Inc., 1954. (A spiritual classic.)

Kodell, Jerome. *The Catholic Bible Study Handbook: A Popular Introduction to Studying Scripture.* Ann Arbor, Mich.: Servant Books, 2001.

Martin, George. *Praying with Jesus: What the Gospels Tell Us About How to Pray.* Chicago: Loyola Press, 2000.

———. *Reading Scripture as the Word of God.* Ann Arbor, Mich.: Servant Books, 1998. (This is its fourth edition. That says something about its popularity and durability.)

Montague, George, T. *Understanding the Bible: A Basic Introduction to Biblical Interpretation.* Mahwah, N.J.: Paulist Press, 1997.

Murphy, Richard, T.A. *Background to the Bible.* Ann Arbor, Mich.: Servant Books, 1978.

Wijngaards, John. *Handbook to the Gospels.* Ann Arbor, Mich.: Servant Books, 1979.

Lectio Divina

Brook, John. *The School of Prayer: An Introduction to the Divine Office for All Christians.* Collegeville, Minn.: The Liturgical Press, 1992.

Casey, Michael. *Sacred Reading: The Ancient Art of Lectio Divina.* Liguori, Mo.: Liguori/Triumph, 1995.

———. *Toward God: The Ancient Wisdom of Western Prayer.* Liguori, Mo.: Liguori/Triumph, 1996.

Deiss, Lucien. *Celebration of the Word.* Collegeville, Minn.: The Liturgical Press, 1993.

Guigo II. *The Ladder of Monks and Twelve Meditations.* Translated by Edmund Colledge and James Walsh. Kalamazoo, Mich.: Cistercian Publications, 1981. (Classic medieval work on *lectio divina.*

Hall, Thelma. *Too Deep for Words: Rediscovering Lectio Divina.* Mahwah, N.J.: Paulist Press, 1988.

Johnson, Maxwell E. *Benedictine Daily Prayer: A Short Breviary.* Collegeville, Minn.: The Liturgical Press, 2005.

Judy, Dwight H. *Christian Meditation and Inner Healing.* New York: The Crossroad Publishing Company, 1991.

Kasl, Ronda, ed., *Giovanni Bellini and the Art of Devotion.* Indianapolis, Ind.: Indianapolis Museum of Art, 2004.

Keating, Thomas. *Invitation to Love*. Rockport, Mass.: Element Books, 1992.

Leclercq, Dom Jean. *The Love of Learning and the Desire for God*. New York: Mentor Omega Books, 1962. (Classic modern work on *lectio divina*.)

Magrassi, Mariano. *Praying the Bible: An Introduction to Lectio Divina*. Collegeville, Minn: The Liturgical Press, 1998.

Masini, Mario. *Lectio Divina: An Ancient Prayer That Is Ever New*. Staten Island, N.Y.: Alba House, 1998.

McDonald, Patrick J. and Claudette M. *Marital Spirituality*. Mahwah, N.J.: Paulist Press, 1999. (Discusses how couples can practice *lectio divina* together.)

Miller, Charles E. *Together in Prayer: Learning to Love the Liturgy of the Hours*. Staten Island, N.Y.: Alba House, 1994.

Muto, Susan Annette. *A Practical Guide to Spiritual Reading*. Petersham, Mass.: St. Bede's Publications, 1994.

Pennington, M. Basil. *Lectio Divina: Renewing the Ancient Practice of Praying the Scriptures*. New York: The Crossroad Publishing Company, 1998.

Rang, Jack C. *How to Read the Bible Aloud*. Mahwah, N.J.: Paulist Press, 1994. (Particularly helpful for those who read the Bible in the liturgy.)

Shannon, William, H. *Seeking the Face of God*. New York: Crossroad, 1990.

Vest, Norvene. *No Moment Too Small*. Kalamazoo, Mich.: Cistercian Publications, 1994.

———. *Bible Reading for Spiritual Growth*. New York: Harper-Collins Publishers, 1993.

Wiederkehr, Macrina. A *Tree Full of Angels: Seeing the Holy in the Ordinary*. San Francisco, CA: Harper & Row, 1988.

Discernment

Green, Thomas H. *Darkness in the Marketplace: The Christian at Prayer in the World*. Notre Dame, Ind.: Ave Maria Press, 1981.

———. *Opening to God*. Notre Dame, Ind.: Ave Maria Press, 1977.

———. *Weeds Among the Wheat: Discernment: Where Prayer and Action Meet*. Notre Dame, Ind: Ave Maria Press, 1988. Notre Dame, Ind.: Ave Maria Press, 1984.

Kelsey, Morton T. *Adventure Inward*. Minneapolis, Minn.: Augsburg Publishing House, 1980.

———. *Discernment: A Study in Ecstacy and Evil*. Minneapolis, Minn.: Augsburg Publishing House, 1978.

Maloney, George A. *The Silence of Surrendering Love: Body, Soul, Spirit Integration*. Staten Island, N.Y.: Alba House, 1986.

Morneau, Robert F. *Spiritual Direction: Principles and Practices*. New York: The Crossroad Publishing Company, 1992.

Valles, Carlos. *The Art of Choosing*. New York: Doubleday, 1989.

Works by the Author

Schultz, Karl A. *The Art and Vocation of Caring for Persons in Pain*. Mahwah, N.J.: Paulist Press, 1994.

———. *Bearing the Unbearable: Coping with Infertility and Other Intimate Suffering: Biblical Meditations and Contemporary Applications Using Lectio Divina*. Ann Arbor, Mich.: Nimble Books, 2007.

———. *Becoming Community: Biblical Meditations and Applications in Modern Life*. New York: New City Press, 2007.

———. *Calming the Stormy Seas of Stress*. Winona, Minn.: St. Mary's Press, 1998.

———. *The How-To Book of the Bible*. Huntington, Ind.: Our Sunday Visitor, 2004.

———. *Job Therapy*. Pittsburgh: Genesis Personal Development Center, 1996.

———. *Journaling with Moses and Job*. Boston: St. Paul Books and Media, 1996.

———. *Nourished by the Word: A Dialogue with Brother Andrew Campbell, O.S.B., on Praying the Scriptures and Holistic Personal Growth* (audiocassette). Notre Dame, Ind.: Ave Maria Press, 1994.

———. *Personal Energy Management: A Christian Personal and Professional Development Program*. Chicago: Loyola University Press, 1994.

———. *Personal Energy Manager Rainbow Planner™*, Pittsburgh: Genesis Personal Development Center, 1996.

———. *Pope Paul VI: Christian Virtues and Values*. New York: Crossroad Publishing Company, 2007.

———. *Where Is God When You Need Him?: Sharing Stories of Suffering With Job and Jesus*. Staten Island, N.Y.: Alba House, 1992.

Schultz, Karl A., and Loreen Hanley Duquin. *The Bible and You*. Huntington, Ind.: Our Sunday Visitor, 2004.

The above books, along with audiotapes, CDs, and DVDs containing the author's presentations on *lectio divina* and other biblical spirituality and personal-growth subjects can be ordered from Genesis Personal Development Center, 3431 Gass Avenue, Pittsburgh, PA, 15212-2239. The e-mail address is karlaschultz@juno.com, and the Web site is karlaschultz.com. The phone number is (412) 766-7545.

About the Author

Karl A. Schultz is one of the world's most innovative and prolific authors and teachers of *lectio divina* and biblical spirituality. He is an acknowledged pioneer in the integration of Catholic biblical scholarship and spirituality with personal development, pastoral care, and gender identity and communications. He has discussed his work on numerous television and radio programs, including several EWTN television programs. He gives *lectio divina*-based programs on St. Joseph and John Paul II's Theology of the Body to men's groups and general audiences across the country.

Schultz has published books on therapeutic and pastoral-care applications of *lectio divina* to the book of Job, human suffering, and care-giving, and has presented "Job Therapy" workshops in a variety of retreat, parish, health-care, and conference environments. His "Building Up the Human" program was approved by the Pennsylvania Nurses Association for R.N. accreditation. Schultz has also written books on applications of *lectio divina* to stress and time management, journaling, wellness and potential fulfillment, infertility and intimate conflict resolution, Christian community, and the teachings of Pope Paul VI and Pope John Paul II.

Information on Schultz's books, tapes, CDs, DVDs, retreats, and presentations can be found on his Web site, karlaschultz.com, or by contacting Genesis Personal Development Center at (412) 766-7545. The e-mail address is karlaschultz@juno.com, and the street address is 3431 Gass Ave., Pittsburgh, PA 15212-2239.

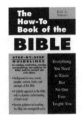

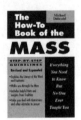